Saint Chaldean

Ancient History of Caledonia

Saint Chaldean

Ancient History of Caledonia

ISBN/EAN: 9783337329907

Printed in Europe, USA, Canada, Australia, Japan

Cover: Foto ©ninafisch / pixelio.de

More available books at **www.hansebooks.com**

ANCIENT HISTORY OF CALEDONIA.

WRITTEN BY

St. CHALDEAN, and the other Saints
of the Chaldean Faith,

And chiefly by the JOHNSTONES, who held the Royal
Pen for Many Hundred Years.

TRANSLATED FROM THE LATIN
By THE REV. DUNCAN M'GREGOR, R. C. PASTOR, LOCHABER.

WITH A COPIOUS INDEX.

PUBLISHED BY
JOHN M'LAREN, SEAMAN, DUNNING.

ENTERED AT STATIONERS HALL.

CONTENTS.

———o———

	PAGES
INTRODUCTORY	1-2
The Israelites being oppressed by the Egyptians, several tribes escape to the Desert—They arrive in Greece, and found the City of Troy	3-4
Dispute with the Greeks, and Siege of Troy—Escape of Lazarus and Daniel with their households—Destruction of Troy	5-8
Arrival and Settlement at Carthagena	8
Prophecy of Lazarus—Deaths of Lazarus and Daniel—Accession of Daniel II. as Prince	9-10
Departure from Carthagena—Self-sacrifice of the Queen	11
Arrival in Sicily—Death of the Prince, and Accession of Daniel III.—Building of Troy East	12
Departure of the faithful, and Destruction of the rebellious and their city	13-14
Arrival in Gaul	14
Death of Daniel III., and Election of Daniel IV.	15
Origin of the M'Intyres	16
Departure of the faithful from Gaul, and Destruction of the remainder—Origin of the Waldenses	18
Arrival in Caledonia	19
Laws of the Altar	20
Founding of Montrose by Daniel and Lazarus—M'Intyre goes to Kinclaven	21-22
Death of Daniel IV., and Accession of Daniel V.	22
Parting of Daniel and Lazarus	23-24
Founding of Dundee by the M'Larens	25
Death of Daniel V. and Election of his son, David I.	27
Donald Grim (founder of the Grahams) rebels against his father David I., who for the sake of peace retires to Port David	28-29
Prophecy of the Messiah by St. Lawrence the Sixth	33
First Appearance of the Romans	34
Invasion by the Romans under Suspacia	35
A Fortress built at Snowton, or Stirling, by the Romans	36
The Romans encounter great hardships, and after many delays encounter the Caledorians at the Battle of Dulganross, where they are defeated—Prince Donald killed in the battle	37-42
Battle of Blairnroar—(Origin of the Roys or M'Roys)—Retreat of the Romans	43-45
Settlements of the Lennoxes, M'Alpins or M'Gregors, Waldenses or Halls, M'Kays, N-ishes or M'Neishes, Rivens, Blythes, &c.	46-47
Building of Abernethy, Lochleven Castle, and Milnathort	48
Founding of the Scots nation—Fergus crowned first king	ib.
Second Roman Invasion—Fife laid waste—Battle of Ardargie—The two sons of Donald II. and other nobles taken prisoners	49
Battle of Lanark	50-51
Fate of the noble prisoners—Cruelties of the Romans to the Nazarenes	52-63

CONTENTS.

	PAGES
The Jews rebel against the Roman power—The Caledonian royal prisoners sent as slaves to the Roman army besieging Jerusalem	54
Finding of Solomon's Crown by James M'Laren—Destruction of Jerusalem	55
Return of the Royal Slaves, with St Chaldean—Prophecy of St. Canaan—Martyrdom of St. Canaan and Murdoch	56-57
Miracles and Prophecies by St. Chaldean—Defeat of the Romans, and their subsequent destruction by a plague	60-61
Donald the Slave, first crowned king of Caledonia—Rapid spread of the Chaldean faith	61-62
Death of Donald III., and Accession of Kenneth I.	62
Destruction of the Roman army in Adamsdale—Remainder driven across the Forth—Division of the new territory	63
Incursion by the Fenians and Romans—Their Defeat by the Caledonians	64
Laws of the Chaldean faith	65
Prophecies of St. M'Isaac	66-67
Foundation of the Erskines	68
Treaty between Donald IV. and Kenneth II. of Fife—Origin of the M'Farlanes and the M'Murrays or Morrisons	69-70
Discovery of Coal and Iron	ib.
Invasion of Fife by the Romans—King Kenneth killed—How the Crown was saved—Defeat of the Romans by the Caledonians at Gask	70-71
Union of Scotland with Caledonia	72
Treaty between Caledonia and the Romans and English—Union with Fife	73
Danish Invasion—How the women of Caledonia kept a secret, and saved their country	74-75
Pursuit of the Danes—Battles of Isaac's Ferry, Mullbowie, Dingwall, Killearn, Loch Broom, and Glenelg	75-77
Grants in the north to M'Kay, the Earl of Ross, Neish, the M'Intyres, &c.	77-78
Invasion of Fife by the Normans, and founding of St. Andrews—Battle of Bargona—Bravery of Daft Donald, founder of the Douglases	79-80
Death of the king—Accession of David II., his folly and death—Accession of Donald IV.	81
Finding of the Crown at Kinfauns	82
Eruption of the Normans into Fife	ib.
Destruction of St Andrews by Earthquake	83
Rise and Spread of the Romish faith	84
Unsettled state of the Lowlands	85
How the Scots and the Druids were treated by the King	86-87
New Roman Invasion—Its disastrous result—Capture of the Roman Fleet in the Clyde—St. Columba	87-89
New Campaign against the Romans—Battle of Glendevon—Failure of the Romans	89-90
Origin of the Fenians—Death of King Donald	90
Accession of David III.—War with the Fenians—Battle of Lochaber	91
Settlements in the North of the Erskines, M'Intoshes, M'Donalds, Stewarts, Rivens, M'Intyres, M'Larens, and Raiths	91-92
Origin of the M'Nabs—Invention of the Water Mill	92
Invasion of Skye by the Normans—Battle of Erskine's Plains—Dispute between Erskine and the king	93-95
Conquest of Mull by M'Lean—Great Battle	96-98

CONTENTS.

	PAGES
War with the Fenians—Clery's Defeat—Battle of Strathblane or Fintry	98-104
Death of David III., and Accession of Donald V.—Regency of Kenneth M Alpin	104
Renewal of the War with the Fenians—Battle of Kilwinning—The Fenians driven out of Scotland—Division of their Territory	104-107
King Donald and the Extortionate Boatman—Donald's Death and Accession of Kenneth II.	107-108
Another Roman Invasion—Desertion of the Waldenses to the Caledonians—Great Battle	108-109
Invasion by the Britons—Desertion to the Caledonians of Loudon and Lauder—Great Battle	110-111
Death of Kenneth II.—Election of Donald VI.	112
Another Invasion by the Britons—Their Defeat—Cession of the country to Scotland, from York northwards	112-113
Saxon Invasion—Conquest of Scotland to the Forth	113-114
Renewal of the War by the Caledonians—The Saxons driven beyond the Tweed	115
Invasion of Fife by the Danes and Normans—Battle of Balgona—Battle of Kilconquhar	116-118
Accession of David IV.—A quiet Reign—Accession of Donald VII.	119-120
Catholic Religion in the Western Isles—Its destruction by the Norwegians	120-121
King Donald's Death—Accession of Malcolm I.—Intended Attack of the English Frustrated—Malcolm's Death	121-122
Accession of Donald VIII.---Priestcraft and Witchcraft---The King's Death	122-123
Accession of Malcolm II.---His troubled reign and Death	123
Accession of Duncan I.---His Vigorous Reign---The Monk's Medicine	123-124
Murder of Duncan by Macbeth, who usurps the throne---Insurrection of M'Duff against Macbeth---Combat between Macbeth and M'Duff at Dunsinane, when Macbeth is killed	124-125
Accession of Malcolm III. (Canmore)---Removal of the King to Auchterarder---The King and the Brewer	125-126
Dispute with England—Invasion of England---The King killed by a Monk---Usurpation by Donald Bain	126
Accession of Duncan II.---His Murder---Anarchy in the country	ib.
Invasion by the English---Edmund crowned---Persecution of the Chaldeans---Battle of Killin---Battle of Dunning---M'Duff killed	128
Fierce Persecutions of the Chaldeans---More Demands by the English, and Preparation for War---A Truce	129
Return of the Exiles from France under Alexander, the King's Uncle, and great muster of the Chaldeans	ib.
Battle of Luncarty---Flight of Edmund---Alexander made King---His Death	130
Accession of David V.---War with England---David killed in battle	ib.
Short reign of Malcolm IV.---Accession of William the Lion	ib.
War with England---Capture of the King---His Abdication in favour of his brother, Alexander II.---Progress of the Church of Rome---Death of the King	131
Accession of Alexander III., the last of the M'Donald kings---Restoration of the Chaldean faith	ib.
Threatened Triple Invasion---Battle of Largs---Battle of Glammis---Plunder of the North of England by Douglas	131-132
Murder of Alexander III.---Numerous claims to the crown---Renewed banishment of St. Johnstone	133

INTRODUCTORY.

———o———

I THINK it necessary to state how I became possessed of the original copy of the "Ancient History of Caledonia." I was a sailor on board a man-of-war. Returning in 1842, I was one day sent on Store Duty to the Tower of London. One of my shipmates calling me by name, a gentleman who heard him came to me and said—" Am I like Jock at the fair—are there more M'Larens here than me ?" I answered that I was a M'Laren. We became very intimate. He was Master Gunner at the Tower, by name David M'Laren. I remained there all night; and the topic of conversation happening to fall upon nationality, he informed me that he had seen a book in the shop of a Jew in Petticoat Lane, with the word " Chaldea" marked upon it. Through curiosity I went along with him to see it. What he called the book turned out to be a large roll of written skins, not very well preserved, there being holes here and there, and the writing in many places injured by damp. An oaken box which had contained the roll, attracted my attention. It was lined with copper, and had outside on the lid a great many ornaments in the same metal, including a large lion rampant with a sword in its paw. I offered him a sum of money for the box, but he would not part with it until he had first removed the mounting from it. I then offered him a piece of money for the book, which he refused ; but when I left he followed after me with it, insisting that I should take it at the price offered, and to avoid being mobbed, I paid the book, got possession of it, and left. After returning home I tried several clergymen with it, but received no encouragement, until I met with the Rev. Duncan M'Gregor, Roman Catholic Priest, Lochaber. He told me it was the "Ancient History of Caledonia." He translated it from the ancient Latin, in which it was written, into the Gælic language, as I expected from the nature of the book that it would command a greater sale in that language. From various causes it never was printed in Gælic, but from this translation, I have now got it translated into the English language, the original document being completely destroyed during the first translation by the means taken to make the writing legible.

I was in Lord Rollo's employment, on his estate of Duncrub, near Dunning, about the year 1862. I told his Lordship of the former existence of a tower on his estate, which I knew of from the "History." Becoming interested, he made enquiries on the subject, but the oldest men in the neighbourhood had never heard of it. He then ordered a search to be made under my direction, which was successful in laying bare the foundations of the tower. Several other statements in this History are proved by recent discoveries—for example, the sinking of St. Andrews has been verified by the fishermen, who have discovered walls and other remains three miles out at sea. The prophecies of St. M'Isaac are partly fulfilled.

The original writings from which this history is translated are believed to have been carried away by Edward I., along with the Marble Chair and Jacob's Pillow, upon which the Caledonians crowned their kings at Scone Palace.

JOHN M'LAREN.

ANCIENT HISTORY OF CALEDONIA.

---o---

AFTER the death of Pharaoh who loved Joseph, the King of Egypt and his rulers saw that the Hebrews prospered more than the Egyptians, that their fields and their vines were more fruitful and pleasant, and also that their wives and daughters were more fair and beautiful than their own. Pharaoh the king then made a law that all those who did not bow down the knee to the Bull, and offer sacrifices upon the King's altar were to be double tithed and their children brought into slavery, which grieved the Hebrews very much ; but they still remembered their God, and went to the desert and offered sacrifice to the God of Bethel. Pharaoh then, being wroth at this, brought all the Hebrews under slavery. The Egyptian slaves got straw to make their bricks ; but the Hebrews had to collect stubble, and make the same number of bricks as the Egyptians, which made their task very grevious to bear ; but they still trusted that God would deliver them from bondage. Then king Pharaoh was enraged, and ordered all the Hebrew children to be slain when they were born. This caused several of the tribes of the Hebrews to draw together, who never defiled themselves among the Egyptians. They then departed into the desert, and withdrew themselves from among them. Pharaoh the king, being wroth, pursued them into the desert with horses and chariots. The Israelites, seeing Pharaoh's hosts at hand, cried to the God of Bethel to deliver them from the hand of their enemy. Then the God of Heaven raised a storm of wind and sand, mountains high, so that they could not find them, and afterwards left them to wander through the desert of Assyria, chiefly living upon fruit. The king of Greece, observing encampments, and being at war with the Egyptians and Assyrians, sent an ambassador to enquire if they had broken the truce that had been made; but they found nothing but working men of crafty work, namely, copper, brass, dyeing and weaving, and also brick-making. The King then, finding they were Hebrews, despatched an Hebrew interpreter, whom they told that they were no rebellious people— that they were under the necessity of fleeing from Egypt to the desert, from the oppression and cruelty of Pharaoh. The Hebrew servant returned and told the king of Greece that they were not men of war, but were working men or craftsmen of Egypt. The king, being pleased with such good news, sent his servant again, telling them to pitch their tents in any plain in his dominions where they pleased—telling them at the same time that they could worship their own God after their own fashion.

The Hebrews then built an altar to the Lord, and offered sacrifice for His great deliverance in saving them from the hands of the Egyptians. The king of Greece visited their camps with his Hebrew servant, telling them to build a city and fortify themselves against their enemies, whoever they might be. They having confidence in this king of Greece, and seeing that the Lord's hand was in their deliverance, commenced to build the city of Troy. The materials of which this city was built were bricks made of clay. This clay was dug to make a canal round the whole city, with draw-bridges to draw up at any time for securing them from their enemies. The work went on so rapidly that they soon found themselves in a fortified position. And as the population increased, so did the city enlarge, the building going on with much vigour; and at the same time the other tradesmen were employed at their own trades, supplying the other nations around them with purple, scarlet, and fine linen, and war instruments of brass, copper, and iron. This surprised the king of Egypt very much, he having laboured under the impression that all the Hebrews were consumed in the mountains of sand (which nearly destroyed the Egyptians); but these had rather served as a protection to the Hebrews.

The king of Greece gave every encouragement to the Hebrews. So much did he adhere to their ways that he was almost persuaded to worship their God ; but owing to his rulers being worshippers of the Horse, they would not allow the king to turn from his former principle, namely, worshipping the Horse, as the priests persuaded the king if he would turn from worshipping the Horse (as that was the god of the Grecians in those days), that his chargers would not face the battle nor enter into the war chariots. Still, the king's heart was with the Hebrews, and he allowed them to go on pilgrimage to the tops of the highest mountains to worship the God of Heaven for his great deliverance of them from the cow-worshippers of Egypt and the tyranny of Pharaoh, which was their custom to do once a year. This was their custom for several hundreds of years, until a war fell out between Greece and Assyria. The Hebrews then refused their young men to go to war ; neither would they allow their daughters to be given in marriage to the uncircumcised Gentiles, unless they would consent to be circumcised and offer seven years' sacrifice in worshipping the God of Bethel. Afterwards one of the Grecian princes fell wroth with the inhabitants of Troy, properly called the Trojans. There was born to one of the princes of Troy, a daughter that excelled in beauty and virtue all the Grecian nation. The prince of the Grecians offered her his hand in marriage, but was refused by the laws of the altar. He then besieged the City of Troy with rage, and drove them into the city, thinking he would make them surrender from hunger ; but they cried to the Lord, and H heard their cry and was pleased to send shoals of fish of all kinds ; but the sturgeon was considered the best fish, and therefore it was chosen for sacrifice on the altar. The turtle doves and pigeons were also innumerable round the city ; they also made use of them for food, being also offered for sacrifice. The wild bee was also very plentiful, supplying them with honey. They lived there in comfort, while their enemies were encamped round the city, suffering many privations. But the young generation arose, and new rulers refused to offer the sacrifices with the sturgeon ; for, as it was the best fish, they wished to keep it for themselves, and offer other fish to the Lord. They also refused to give the poor, the widow, the fatherless, and the orphan, their proper share—neither the quality nor the quantity which they took for themselves. They began to refuse to keep the Jubilee, the Sabbath of the land, which occurred once in seven years. The custom was that if any one sold a possession, they could have it again in the year of Jubilee; but that they began to refuse to do, and went contrary to the law of God. They also claimed the honey, the turtle doves and pigeons, of which the Lord said that every one was to share alike, both priests and people. The Lord was then pleased to open the eyes of Lazarus, one of the tribe of Levi, a devoted priest of the Lord, and said unto him—" Take unto thee a sturgeon fish, and a pair of turtle doves, and a pair of young pigeons, and offer a peace offering, and a sin offering, and a thanksgiving offering, and say unto the people, 'The Lord, the God of Heaven, hath said unto me, Twice seven years have I provided for your table and furnished it abundantly, and ye have rebelled against me, saith the Lord.' But if they do not repent and return unto me, I will give them up to destruction." But instead of repenting they became more hardened and more rebellious than ever, mocking and scoffing at the servant of the Lord. The God of Heaven began to withhold His mercies from them; the vines and date trees were blasted, and failed in bringing forth fruit; the bees and doves and pigeons failed to supply their wants; and also the fish failed them. The harder the times were, the more they blasphemed the God of Heaven, and persecuted His servants, boasting that their walls had protected them and would protect them still, and wantonly joining in all the abominations of the Gentiles, saying, "The Gentiles dance and make merry, and drink wine, and why not we?—our walls will protect us."

The Lord was then about to bring on the destruction of Troy. He appeared to Lazarus the Levite, and said, "Arise up early in the morning, and call upon those that serve me, and say unto them, 'Arise and depart out of this city; for truly I will destroy it, because they are a rebellious and stiff-necked people, who have hardened their hearts against me and my servants. Therefore, arise at the twelfth glass, at midnight, when the watches are shifted on the towers, and come to the twelfth gate, which lieth toward the sea.'" And a great many of them went home to their own houses when they heard the word of the Lord, and doubted the word of the prophet. And out of the great multitude of the inhabitants of the city there were only about one hundred souls that did according to the word of the Lord—the ancient ruler Daniel and all his household, and Lazarus the Levite and all his household.

The boats were all arranged at the seaside, and the scanty provisions that the city could afford were brought for their use. They also took on board Jacob's Pillow and the Marble Chair which was the seat of their prince or chief. They then departed from Troy, leaving the enemies of God to their fate.

Immediately thereafter, Satan filled the hearts of the Gentiles with guile, so that they prepared a large wooden horse, and put two men inside of it. They also took a man and cut off his nose, and made him all wounds over his body They then fled from the city, leaving all property and goods behind them. The Trojans saw next morning that the Gentiles had all fled; but seeing this wounded man standing by the side of the wooden horse, he told them that the Gentiles had all fled, and that they had used him thus when he would not go along with them; and he said to them, "I will tell you the whole truth of the judgments of God that befell them." This man also told them that this (the wooden horse) was a god sent down from the gods above, for the love they bore to Fair Helen of Troy. Then, instead of the Trojans giving thanks to the God of Bethel, they filled themselves with wine and strong drink, and made themselves riotous, dancing round this horse. They then sought to kill the chief ruler and their prophet Lazarus; but found that they had departed from the city. That very night, while they lay drunken on the streets, the Gentiles came back, and the two men that were in the wooden horse opened the gates of the city and gave them entrance, and with fire and sword they destroyed the City of Troy; but at the same time the Lord was avenged of the Gentiles. There had been concealed beneath the chief synagogue some *devil's fire*, as the Grecians called it in those days, with which the Trojans defended their city. They took their wooden horse and put it upon the altar of the God of Bethel; but at the very moment when they crowded into the synagogue the Lord was pleased to consume them with fire from heaven, which caused the *devil's fire* to explode, and caused the destruction of every man within the synagogue that was worshipping the horse.

The ancient Trojans were then scattered through all the Grecian nation, and those that were left of the Greeks occupied Troy; but the Lord visited it with high winds, so that all the fertile lands were scorched and turned into barrenness. He also visited the city with an earthquake, and sunk it with all its kings and rulers, ten fathoms below the level of the sea. The spot where the city stood is now called the Bay of Pechoi. Such was the end of Troy with all its splendour.

Those who left the city under persecution were in sight of the destruction of it all the time, and were enabled to glorify the God of Bethel for all His goodness to them in delivering them from the same destruction.

The Lord caused a mighty wind, and drove their boats ashore upon the Island of Carthagena, which was governed by a queen, whom they called their goddess. Immediately, the young men were ordered to go and collect stones, which were neither to be hewn nor cut, to build an altar to the God of Bethel. There were twelve stones laid round the outside circle, to represent the twelve tribes of Israel. Early the next morning, Lazarus the Levite arose, washed and anointed himself, and finding a lamb and a kid near the altar, he offered the lamb for a peace offering, and the kid for a sin offering, and a pair of young turtles for a thanksgiving offering. They at this time found great favour in the eyes of the queen, who allotted them a piece of ground, which they cultivated, planting vines, and the Lord blessed the work of their hands. For many years they kept the rules of the altar very strictly. The Sabbath was also kept (which occurs once in seven years), and every man got land according to the number of his family. They were at this time ruled by their own prince Daniel, who occupied the Marble Chair.

Lazarus at this time being an old man, called unto him the rulers and elders of the people, and said unto them—" Regard the words of the Lord, and judge the people justly ; defraud not the widow, the fatherless, and the orphan ; shift not thy neighbour's land-mark, and covet not anything thine that belongeth to thy neighbour ; neither add field to field, nor deal unjustly one toward another ; for cursed is he that enlargeth his wealth against the law of God." He then called his own son Lazarus, and said—" Teach thou the people according to the law of the Lord, as I have taught you, lest the people sin, and the Lord require it of your hand ; for the Lord will hold you responsible for your charge, if not faithful. Great tribulation and persecution shall befall you, but fear not. There will multitudes of the people backslide to the Gentiles, but do thou not depart from the laws of the Lord ; for you shall soon be removed from this land to find another home. Take courage then from the Lord ; for He shall keep thee as the apple of His eye, as long as thou wilt keep His laws and statutes. The land that the Lord hath prepared for you, ye shall know it; for this shall be a token, that the blood of your chief shall stain the shore before your feet shall tread it. Ye shall stand together and not separate ; but it will be the third generation from the present till ye possess the land that the Lord hath prepared for you. Fear not the princes nor powers of the earth, but trust in the God of your fathers." He then called Daniel, the prince and ruler of the people, and the elders, and said to Daniel—" As thou art old and well stricken in years, teach thy son the laws of God, and how to rule His people ; and see that every man gets according to his family. And see that thou drinkest no strong drink, nor dost anything contrary to the laws of the Lord ; for what thou hast under thine hand is not thine own, but belongeth to the Lord ; and if thou dealest not justly, the Lord shall cast thee off for ever." So the old saint Lazarus yielded up the ghost, being one hundred and twenty years of age, and the people mourned for him three times seven days. And when the days of mourning were ended, his son, who was also called Lazarus, washed himself, and anointed his head with oil, and went in unto the altar and offered a lamb for his original sin ; and he spake unto the people, saying, "See that the one lay not a stumbling-block before the other, for so spake the law of the Lord. Mothers, teach your children in all the ways of the altar, so that they go not astray among the Gentiles."

The customs of the people were that the betrothed women wore the blue veil and three-cornered napkin, with white border; the married women wore the blue veil and four-cornered napkin; the virgins wore the white veil, so that they might be distinguished from the other women, and that no man might lust after them, to bring a reproach upon the Lord; the widows wore the thick black veil. The custom of the widow was to marry the nearest kinsman of her husband; and if she bore no children to her first husband, the first child of the second husband was to be named after the first, so that his name might not be cut away. The people lived very strictly according to the law, as it was their belief that if they committed sin they would die. They went on so living in the fear of the Lord, and the Lord blessed all the labours of their hands, and their fields and vines prospered before the Lord. This grieved the Gentiles very much, seeing them so prosperous.

Daniel, being an old man, and very much cast down at the death of Lazarus his prophet, was taken ill. He then called his son Daniel, who was named after himself, and said—"I charge thee, rule the people as I have been enabled to do, and prepare against the day of your departure out of this land; for the word of the Lord shall come to pass, as the prophet said. Cause the people to give one-tenth of the produce of the land, to be laid up in store. Prepare all your boats and have them in readiness for those who will follow thee. Fear not, for the Lord will direct thee where thou shalt go." So Daniel slept with his fathers, and the people mourned for him three times seven days. And when the days of mourning were ended, his son, who was also called Daniel, the second ruling prince, washed himself, and anointed his head with oil, and was placed in the Marble Chair; and Jacob's Pillow was used as a footstool to all the princes that have ruled since they left Egypt. The priest Lazarus then went in to the altar, and offered unto the Lord a lamb for Daniel's original sin.

This lamb was a type of the promised Messiah, who was to carry away all the sins of the world.

At this time there was a young queen of the Gentiles who sought the young prince Daniel in marriage, promising to worship his God; but he refused her offer. After this, the rulers, elders, and priests of Vulcan (the god whom the Gentiles worshipped at that time) fell wroth with the Trojans, and told them that if they did not worship their god they must leave the land, or war would be proclaimed against them. At this, Daniel was sore perplexed, and called all the rulers and elders together, with Lazarus. This was the prophecy that was foretold. They then agreed to depart and leave the land upon a certain day appointed. The boats were all in readiness, when an unruly band of Gentiles, chiefly of women, coming to destroy their boats by fire, were observed by prince Daniel, and he cried—

"Cease, ye matrons, why so destroy
The last remains of poor unfortunate Troy?"

So, upon the day appointed, all the faithful followers of the God of Bethel came to the shore to depart. The Marble Chair and Jacob's Pillow were put on board the prince's boat, and all the other boats were stored with provisions. A great number of the Trojans, however, rather than leave their fields and vineyards, went with the Gentiles and became worshippers of Vulcan. The queen then ordered a very high scaffold to be erected, and a large bonfire to be placed close by it, so that she might see the departure of the Trojans. Then Lazarus came to the shore, and brought a pair of turtle doves to offer as a peace offering; and this was to be a token, that whatever way the smoke was to blow, that was the way their boats were to go. So Lazarus went into his own boat, and all the elders of the people with him, and they departed amidst mocking and scoffing by the backsliders of the Trojans and Gentiles. The queen looked and longed after the boats as long as they were in sight, and while the fire was burning at its height she gave a loud cry and flung herself into the flames as a sacrifice to Cupid, for the sake of the Trojan prince Daniel.

During some time the Trojans were tossed upon the sea, not knowing where they were to land; but at last they were driven ashore upon a beautiful country near to the burning mountain of Etna. So they agreed with the rulers of that place for a piece of their country, after which they began to work in their own industrious manner. The inhabitants of the place were astonished when they saw the Trojans worshipping only once in seven days; for they, being idolators, had a god for every day in the week. They asked the Trojans what god they worshipped, and Lazarus craftily told them that it was the God of the sun. They on that account were allowed to remain in this place; for one tribe of the Gentiles worshipped the sun.

The Trojans remained for a long time in this place. It then happened that Daniel, their prince, being an old man, called unto him his son (who was Daniel the third), and Lazarus, and said unto Lazarus—"Put thy hand under my thigh, and thy right foot upon this stone, and swear to me that you will teach the rules of the altar to my son and all the people, lest they all go astray from the laws that I have taught them." He also spoke to his son Daniel, and said—"Remember the laws of the God of Bethel, of Abraham, Isaac, and of Jacob." So Daniel the second slept with his fathers, and his son reigned in his stead, and they mourned for him three times seven days. And when the days of mourning were ended, Daniel washed and anointed himself, and came to Lazarus, who took a lamb and offered it for the original sin of Daniel, and placed him on his father's Marble Chair, and all the congregation came together and blessed him; and Lazarus said to all those assembled—"See that ye all walk in the laws of the Lord, and not mingle amongst the Gentiles. Build no city here; for the prophet hath said that this is not the land that the Lord hath prepared for us." But some of them would have their own way, and began to build a city, and the foundation was laid and partly built. At this time the Gentiles were looking on them with jealousy, seeing them prospering and fortifying a city. This city was called Troy East. Lazarus, however, told them that they were breaking the rules and laws of God, and told them to refrain from dealing with the Gentiles. But some of the young men went among the women of the Gentiles, and joined in their abominations; and they began to exchange their goods for lands, which was contrary to the laws of God. Daniel, being grieved at their behaviour, strictly gave orders that those who were dealing with the Gentiles were not to return to the congregation of the Lord. And Lazarus cried unto the Lord, and the Lord told him to cry to the people and tell them their destruction was at hand, if they did not return and offer sacrifice and repent of their sin. Daniel also said that no one was to build any more, as it was against the prediction of their prophet, who foretold them that the blood of their prince would stain the shore before their feet should tread upon it. Lazarus, being by this time an old man, and much borne down with grief at the rebellion of the people, called unto him his son, Lazarus, who was called after himself and his father, and blessed him, and said—" Be thou anointed of the Lord, and be thou strong as a lion and wise as a serpent; for I am leaving thee among a stiff-necked and rebellious people who will try thee very much." He then called Daniel, the ruling prince of the people, and said—" Prepare thou thy boats, and lay up stores of provision, and whatsoever the people stand in need of; for the day draweth nigh in which thou must leave this land; and be sure that thou leavest behind those who have defiled themselves amongst the Gentiles, for the day of their destruction is at hand." So Lazarus closed his eyes and slept with his fathers, and they mourned for him three times seven days. And when the days of mourning were ended, Lazarus the third arose and washed himself, and anointed his head with oil, and called together the chief ruler, the elders, and all the congregation, and took a lamb, and offered it upon the altar for his original sin. He then told all the congregation to prepare, for the day of vengeance was at hand; and he took water and washed his hands, and said— "I take God and man, moon and stars, as witnesses that I am clear of the guilt and sin of these people who have mingled with the Gentiles, in giving their daughters for wives, offering sacrifices on their altars, eating their unclean food, and in buying and selling land, which it was not legal for them to do." Then the Gentiles and the Jews that were joined to them were wroth with Daniel and his people, and conspired to capture their young children for slaves; but the Lord opened the eyes of the prophet, and said unto him—" Get up, and take with thee all those who have kept my laws, and leave this place, and I will direct thee where thou shalt go." So the prophet called all the people, rulers, and elders together, and said—" Prepare to leave this night, for the Lord will destroy this place." So they all came to the shore; and the Marble Chair and Jacob's Pillow were put on board Daniel's boat. After they had left the shore they beheld the destruction of the city, Troy East. All that remained, or escaped from fire and sword, were sold as slaves by the Gentiles; while the faithful Hebrews were wafted away on the wide ocean, praising the Lord for all his goodness in delivering them from their enemies.

They next landed on the shores of Gaul, which was a most beautiful country. There were few inhabitants in this place, and when they saw the Hebrews they all took flight to the mountains. After arriving in this place they rejoiced and said that they had at last landed on their own country; but the prophet told them it was not so. Lazarus then ordered the young men to go to the mountains and bring stones to build an altar for the Lord, which stones were neither to be hewn nor broken, but just as the Lord had formed them. The altar was then built in the usual way, with the twelve stones round the outside circle, representing the twelve tribes of Israel. Lazarus and all the elders of the congregation went in to the altar, and offered a lamb for a sin offering, a kid for a peace offering, and a pair of young pigeons for a thanksgiving offering. Then all the people arose, and praised the Lord for all his mercies. Then Daniel divided the land to every man according to the number of his household, according to the law of the Lord. At the end of every seventh year was the year of release, in which whatever was bonded or borrowed was released, according to the law—this year was called the Sabbath of the land. The people lived very strictly in accordance with the laws for many a long year.

David, the brother of the ruling prince, died and left a young widow with a young family. The spirit of jealousy then entered the prince, and he coveted the widow's vineyard and fields, they being situated near by his own. He offered her in exchange four times more land; but that which he offered was far removed from her present possessions. With great grief the widow and her young family were compelled to depart, leaving her former possessions, her fields and vineyards, behind. Daniel's oldest son was seized with a severe illness and died. Daniel then went to enquire at the priest, Lazarus, what he was to do, telling him his oldest son was dead, and he was afraid the other members of his family would die also. Lazarus told him the sin lay at his own door, inasmuch as he had coveted his brother's widow's fields and vineyards; and he said—"Arise and go on pilgrimage for seventy-seven days, and uncover thy head, so that it may be wet with the dews of heaven, and give back to the widow her fields and vineyards and also half of thine own, to make good the evil thou hast done unto her and her fatherless family; this shalt thou do, lest the Lord cut off thy name for ever from among His people." So the prince did all that the prophet told him; and he brought a ram, the first of his flock, and gave it to the priest, who offered it to the Lord upon the altar for a sin offering, and was there reconciled and brought back to his office. After the death of his son Daniel, there was born to him another son, and he called his name Daniel also. The Lord prospered the child Daniel, and he grew up to be a young man. He had also a brother older than himself, whom they called David, and they both strove for the mastery. So Daniel, their father, being an old man, slept with his fathers, leaving both his sons without either his blessing or counsel. The people mourned for Daniel three times seven days; and when the days of mourning were ended, his two sons went to the priest Lazarus, to enquire what counsel he would give them. The one strove because his name was called Daniel; while the other, David, strove because of his birthright. The prophet told each of them to bring a lamb as an offering to the Lord. He then called together the rulers, the elders, and all the people, and said—" Which of these two young men will ye choose for your ruler?" And all the people cried—" We will have Daniel for our prince and ruler."

Then the prophet said—" We will enquire of the Lord by the sacrifices." He then put David's offering upon the altar, as he was the oldest; and the smoke spread over the face of the whole earth round about, so that the Lord did not accept it. He then put Daniel's offering upon the altar, and the smoke ascended to heaven, and all the people cried with a loud voice—" Daniel is the Lord's chosen" The priest anointed Daniel with oil, and set him on the Marble Chair, and his feet upon the Stone, saying—"Thy father hath not blessed thee, nor given thee his counsel; but the Lord hath blessed thee, and shall counsel thee, and shall stand by thee, and be thy God." Then David went away very wroth with his brother, and wished to withdraw or separate from him altogether.

David then took to himself a wife, and separated from his brother Daniel; and he called his firstborn the wright's son, or M'Intyre, as he was a wright himself to his profession. By this time Lazarus was an old man, and knew that his departure was at hand. He called his son Lazarus (being Lazarus the fourth), and said—" This is the third generation from Lazarus the prophet who prophecied that the Lord would provide a land, but it would be the third generation from the present that would possess it. Now this is the third generation from that prophecy, and surely as the Lord hath spoken, his words shall come to pass; and be sure when thou comest to the land that the Lord shall give thee, that thou givest to every man according to the number of his family." He then called Daniel, the prince and chief ruler, and said unto him —" See that thou followest not the footsteps of thy father, in defrauding the widow and the fatherless, and turn not aside to the right nor the left from following the Lord; and see that thou keepest the Sabbath of the land, which is the seventh year and the year of release, when all that is lent or borrowed or defrauded during the year is to be returned." Daniel was then placed in the Marble Chair, and he made Lazarus stand on the Stone Pillow, his left hand round the prince's neck, and his right hand under his thigh, and made him swear that they would have no war, nor depart from the law of the Lord; for there were to be no Gentiles in the land whither they were going, neither was it ever trod by feet of men—nothing but harmony and innocence was to be there. And he said to him—" Be not afraid, but rejoice when thou art encompassed with thine enemies, the Gentiles, for the day draweth nigh in which thou must leave this land and go to the place that the Lord hath prepared for thee; and those that keep the words of the Lord by the mouth of his prophets shall escape the wrath to come, but those that believe not shall be left to be scattered to the four winds of heaven. After thou hast gone to this land that the Lord hath prepared for thee, there shall no enemy disturb thy peace; and if any of thy people disturb another, thou shalt cast them out of the congregation of the Lord, and He shall deal with them according to His righteous judgment; but if the man repent of his sin, thou shalt accept of his sacrifice on the seventh year, and he shall be returned again to the congregation of the Lord." The prophet then took his son to the altar and blessed him, and said—" Cleanse thine heart from covetousness, and be thou the friend of the fatherless, the poor and needy—as the God of heaven is their friend, be thou also their friend on earth, and if any one borrow of the widow, let them return it fourfold; and see also that thou offerest sacrifice every seventh day for the sin of the people, for the Lord will reserve a seed to serve Him in the land whither thou shalt go." So Lazarus the third closed his eyes, and slept with his fathers, and they mourned for him three times seven days; and when the days of mourning were ended, Lazarus the fourth rose and washed and anointed himself, and took a lamb and offered it upon the altar for his original sin. He then called unto him the chief rulers and all the elders of the congregation, and said unto them—" This is not the land that we shall dwell in, but the Lord shall not delay in performing His promise; so let every man lay up in store the tenth of his produce against the day of his departure." Some scoffed at the words of the prophet, and began to their usual duties, taking no notice of what he had told them, saying—" There are no enemies near us, and no appearance of anything like what the prophet hath said." At this time the Lord caused a great dearth to spread over all the land of the Gentiles, so much so that they had to range over mountains and dales seeking provision; and from the tops of these mountains they saw the valley of Gaul, with its vines and fruits, and pleasant fields of wheat and corn; and immediately the covetous hearts of the Gentiles yearned to be in possession of them. They then raised a mighty army of men, headed by Francetenous; but the Lord had not forgotten His faithful servant, Lazarus, for he appeared to him by night, and said unto him—" Call all thy faithful followers together, and tell them to prepare to leave this place, for the enemy is about to destroy it." Lazarus then brought a lamb, and offered it upon the altar for the sins of the people; for they could not enter the presence of the Lord without a bloody sacrifice, being typical of the great sacrifice, the Messiah. Then immediately all those who believed the words of the prophet prepared themselves, and carried all their provisions to the shore, their boats all being in readiness. Daniel, the ruling prince, ordered that every boat was to hold a certain number of people, and also a certain quantity of goods. The Marble Chair and Jacob's Pillow were put on board the prince's boat, and the priests and elders occupied Lazarus' boat. The unbelievers went to follow after their usual employment, and took no notice of all that was doing; but the sun had not set ere the dreadful alarm of the approaching enemy was heard. The people then ran to and fro seeking shelter, but finding none. Some ran to the shore, but the boats were gone; some ran to the mountains, some to the wilderness (these were afterwards called the faithful Waldenses); some fell by the sword, and others were sold as slaves. So all was made waste by the rude hand of the Gentiles; but the people of God, by this time, were driven within sight of Wales. The prince hoisted up his colours of scarlet and blue; but the inhabitants made them no welcome. Many of them, however, came round the shore—men of larger stature than they had ever seen, wearing nothing but foreskins painted from the bark of trees. The prince, believing they were still Gentiles, ordered his people to steer their boats away as quick as possible. At this time an occurrence took place which grieved them very much. One of the boats of the household of Lazarus was driven away or lost, so that they could give no account of it whatever. Soon after this a murmuring arose among the people; for M'Intyre thought himself rightful heir to the Marble Chair, and stirred up strife against Daniel and Lazarus—so much so, that the M'Intyre party would have willingly steered back their boats to Gaul; for their universal cry was—" Better for us had we been enslaved in Gaul than to die here with thirst. We have corn in abundance, but we cannot grind it for want of water." The prophet then ordered one of the young men to cast over his hook. He did so and caught a sturgeon, which the prophet offered as a sacrifice on Jacob's Pillow, on board the prince's boat; and he raised his eyes to heaven, and cried unto the Lord to send rain, and immediately rain came in torrents, so that they had to bale their boats to keep them from sinking. Then they filled all their vessels with water sufficient to supply them till they landed on the promised land. They were afterwards surrounded with a heavy fog, so that they were becalmed; and Lazarus called all the boats together, and spake unto the people, and told them to put an end to all their mourning, for they were near the shore, and the first man that would land on that shore would be their prince and ruler. So next morning the sun shone with great brilliancy, and all the people cried out—" The land! the land!" So M'Intyre and Daniel strove with great vehemence to reach the shore; but the boats of Saint Lazarus strove not, so that M'Intyre was like to make to the shore first. Daniel seeing this, immediately clutched a hatchet for cleaving wood, and laid his left hand upon a block, and cleaving it, caught it by the fingers with his right hand, and pitched it upon the shore, and cried out with a loud voice—" I take God and man, moon and stars, as witnesses that my flesh, blood, and bones reach the shore before M'Intyre." So all the people cried—" Daniel is our prince; and surely this is the prophecy of Lazarus the First, that led our fathers from Troy."

So Lazarus and all the people landed; and Lazarus ordered the young men to gather stones to build an altar, so that they

might offer a thank offering to the Lord before th
eat or drink. They got a pair of pigeons from c
and offered them upon the altar, giving praise an
God of Bethel for all his manifold kindness to the
the young men prepared their bows and arrows,
forest to provide venison, which was very plentifu
went to search for water, and in their search the
river in which was abundance of fish, which river
Esk, or river of fish. Then Daniel and Lazarus
a suitable place to build the House of God, whil
set to work. Lazarus, as was his wont, assemble
together for worship on the seventh day, and sa
"This surely is the land that the Lord hath pro
all the prophecy is fulfilled. Let every man go an
himself and his family, for the land is before the
every man deal justly, and covet nothing belongi
bour." He then called together all the fathers an
people, and said unto them—"I charge thee, fathe
that thou shalt teach thy children in all the statut
the Lord, as I have told thee; and see that tho
one that teacheth the law of the Lord."

The laws of the altar were as follows:—

If any man insulted a young virgin before
original sin offering, the man was taken out and
by the woman, so that his name might perish f
people. If a man insulted a virgin who was come
found illegitimate, she was examined before th
congregation; and if they found her ignorant of
altar, the father and mother and elder were cal
and deprived of the benefit and privilege of the a
and forest, for seven years, that they might be an
congregation; but if they found out that she had
in the laws of the altar, she was brought along
before the congregation, and rebuked for seven
woman was ordered to take off the white veil, so
be distinguished from the rest of virgins, while t

allowed to wear any badge belonging to his clan during that time, but if they shewed works meet for repentance, they were to come at the expiration of seven years, and offer a sin offering; then they were betrothed to each other for twelve months, after which he took her for his wife, and entered again into the congregation of the Lord. If any man coveted his neighbour's wife, or a betrothed virgin, or insulted them in any way, he was cast out from the congregation of the Lord, and had to serve as a servant three times seven years to whomsoever the priest, rulers, and elders appointed him; and if at the end of that time he came back confessing his fault, he was admitted again into the congregation of the Lord. Any man that coveted his neighbour's land, or accused his neighbour falsely, was put out from among the congregation of the Lord, and also lost all benefit of flood and forest; but if at the end of seven years he came to his neighbour and compromised with him, he was again admitted to the congregation of the Lord. This finished the laws of the altar.

They called the name of the first city they established Mantrogen afterwards Montrose; and the shore they first landed on they called Red Head, as blood stained the land.

Then Daniel the prince called all the people together, and said— "This is the rule of the land:—Let no man touch the hind with her young, nor the fish upon the spawn bed, lest the blessing of God be taken from us by touching the unclean. Again, if there be a widow among you, the nearest kinsman to her husband shall look after her rights, and see that she gets her share of fish and venison, and that she have her share by lot, so that there may be no fraud; but if a woman die, and leave her husband and family, the nearest kinswoman shall perform her part in nursing the youngest, and he shall reward her with the produce of his land. Let every man labour on his own land, as it is the Lord's blessing, for the Lord hath said that every man shall eat his bread by the sweat of his brow, and cursed be the man that eateth his bread by the sweat of his neighbour's brow." He then divided to every man his portion of land, according to the number of his family or household; but M'Intyre, wishing to separate from Daniel his brother, by order of the priest got half of his brother's cattle and all that he had. So M'Intyre departed, and took his journey toward the west, and landed at Birnam, where he built an altar. Here M'Intyre's company increased to a great number. His place of abode was Kinclaven; but Lazarus and Daniel still dwelt at Montrose.

Lazarus by this time was an old man, and knowing his time of departure was at hand, he called his young son, Lazarus the Fifth, and said—"My son, the blessing of God and my blessing be upon thee, and see that thou stray not from following the footsteps of thy fathers, and that thou covet not; but let the love of thy God fill thy heart, and do justly to the people; for they shall increase and be a very great nation. For hundreds of years nothing shall annoy or disturb them from serving the Lord, until the blessed Messiah come on earth; but then you may 'expect great tribulation. Then there shall be no pilgrimage nor sacrifice required; for He shall put an end to all by offering himself for the whole world,—fulfilling the office of a Prophet, a Priest and a King." So Lazarus blessed his son and died, and the people mourned for him three times seven days; and when the days of mourning were ended, Lazarus arose, and washed himself, and anointed his head with oil, and went to the altar, and offered a lamb for his original sin, and collected all the people and said unto them—"See that you keep the laws of the Lord, and attend to all the directions of the elders." Daniel, being grieved at the death of Lazarus the prophet, and weighed down with the charge of the people, fell sick; and seeing the time of his departure was at hand, he called unto him his son, and said unto him, "I am going to my fathers, and I charge thee to rule the people rightly, lest thou shalt bring God's wrath upon thee." So Daniel blessed his son and died. Thus died the two patriarchs who led the people into the land that the Lord had prepared for His ancient people. They mourned for Daniel three times seven days, and when the days of mourning were ended, Daniel the Fifth arose and washed himself, and anointed his head with oil, and was set in his father's Marble Chair, with Jacob's Pillow under his feet; and Lazarus the Fifth took a lamb and offered it upon the altar for the original sin of Daniel. He then gathered all the people together, and gave them directions, saying—" You shall walk in the ways of the Lord as ye have been taught. As I am a young man I shall labour my own land, and kill my own venison; but this distinction shall be observed—the arrow of my bow shall have two wickers, the priest's shall have one wicker, and the people shall have a plain arrow. The laws of the forest shall be given on the law month day, or Lammas Day. The young men shall go to the forest, and kill venison, and provide for the old and infirm that are not able to provide for themselves. The widow and the fatherless are to be provided for—every one's share to be given by lot, so that there may be no fraud; the fish are also to be divided in the same manner. If a man and his wife have no family, the nearest kinsman must be taken into the family; and the elders of the congregation will look after them, so that the old people will be well cared for; and the first-born son will be called after the old man, so that his name may not be cut off from the congregation of the Lord."

The custom of dress at this time was, that the priest wore a long black robe; the elders wore a blue robe, girded with a black belt; the young men wore the garb according to their clan; and the women wore a long garb of blue, and head-dresses according to their station.

At this time, Lazarus the Fifth was betrothed to Margaret, the daughter of Daniel the patriarch; and Daniel the Fifth was betrothed to Mary, the daughter of Lazarus the patriarch, who was the chief priest. And when the days of betrothment were at an end each one took home his wife; for it was an abomination in the eyes of the Lord, and against the laws of the altar for a man to have a concudine.

Shortly after this, Lazarus and Daniel held a consultation together. The people of both parties were getting very numerous; and, in order to prevent any quarrel arising among them, Lazarus thought it advisable that he and his people should find a place for themselves. Daniel then said to Lazarus—" Tarry thou with me, and I will send my young men along with your young men, and they will bring us word again. I will direct them by the sun at high noon, so that they may not come in contact with M'Intyre or his people." So the young men went toward the south, burning the heath as they went along, for fear of the serpents, which were very numerous. On the third day from their departure, they came to the sea, and a large mountain by the side of it covered with tall green pine. They also found by the back of this mountain a beautiful river, in which was plenty of fish. So they returned to Daniel and told him all they had seen; after which Lazarus said to Daniel—"Now, I pray thee, let me depart in peace with all my kindred; and as it was with our fathers, so shall it not be with us, on account of the great number of our people." And Daniel said to him—"The people have all their own cattle; but, as for your father and my father, they were sworn never to part." So they lived together and died together and were buried in one sepulchre. Early next morning, Daniel told Lazarus to come forward, and he would divide to him justly in the sight of God and all the elders. He then asked Lazarus to choose the right hand side or the left; and he said—"I will choose the right hand, toward the mountain." Then they drove out the cattle from the fold, and those that went to the right Lazarus' men took for him, while those that went to the left Daniel's men took; but most part went to the right, toward the mountain. And Daniel said to his people—"All the white calves shall be thine, and all the small sheep and goats that we have captured shall also be thine." The native cow was white, with black tongue and black nose.* The native horse was small, and of grey colour. The large deer and roebuck were very plentiful. There was a large black bird called the capercallie, which was very beautiful; and all kinds of ducks frequented the swamps, and black grouse of all sorts were very plentiful. God in his goodness supplied them with the produce of flood and forest in great abundance. They had also the strawberry, crowberry, and blaeberry. The geen tree and the rowan tree were all the fruit trees they found in the country. These fruits were so large at

* It is believed that the last of this species belongs to the Duke of Hamilton.

that time that they made their wines from them in abundance. They brought wheat, corn, and barley with them from Gaul; the women also brought lint seed with them for the purpose of making lining for their dresses, and such like. Daniel then divided all he had in his house with Lazarus; and the sons of Donald and the and the sons Laurence separated.

[The language here is so much changed, that the Hebrew language was almost lost. The names were changed from Daniel to Donald, and his sons belonged to the M'Donald clan; and the name of Lazarus was also changed to Laurence, and his sons were called the M'Laren clan.]

M'Laren and his clan now took their departure, and prince Donald and his young men came a day's journey with them. They then took an oath that the one clan was to help the other at whatever time help might be required. All the festivals and thanksgivings offered to God for his goodness were to be kept yearly by both clans at Saint Laurence's altar, as he was high priest. So the two clans separated without the sound of pibroch, as their hearts were sad at the separation. Then Saint Laurence came to the hill which the young men had found, and told them to get stones, and build an altar to the God of Bethel. It was built in the usual manner, with twelve stones round the outside circle, representing the twelve tribes of Israel; and here Saint Laurence offered a ram for a thanksgiving offering, and a lamb for a sin offering. He then called all his clan around him, and said— "We shall surely call this place the Hill of God." The place is now called Dundee. Then the people began to build a synagogue to the Lord, after which the land was divided among them. Some went northward, some went southward, some went eastward, and some went westward round about the hill. Saint Laurence built his own house near the river, which he called Inverlowrine, now Invergowrie. They all lived in a God-fearing manner, obeying all the laws of God.

Now the grandson of M'Intyre, who rebelled in Gaul, and broke off from Lazarus and Daniel, and went to Birnam, being there oppressed with satrass, or man monkey, of a prodigious size, was forced to leave that place and come to Saint Laurence of Dundee for protection. This race of man monkey lived chiefly on fish. They had no language, but seemed to understand each other by fearful screaming and roaring. They were very mischievous to cattle, and the inhabitants became afraid of them. There was nothing that frightened them except fire; and when the inhabitants heard them near by, they would set fire to the heath to frighten them. Through the course of time, however, they wore back to the forest. When they became familiar with the human species, it was dangerous for the women to go out. Daniel the ruler seeing this, appointed certain days in the week for the young men to go out with their bows and arrows and hunt them down; and they soon got the mastery over them. There was also the wild boar, which was very disgusting to the people. The custom was that if a man went on pilgrimage, and if he happened to meet a satrass, or wild boar, or any unclean beast, he had to return and commence his journey afresh. Their pilgrimage was for many years to the Hill of God, now called Dundee. At this place all the three clans met, and all grievances were settled before any sacrifice was offered. The particular spot on the hill was called the clachan, which means stone; and the reason of this was, that every clan placed a large stone there for their chiefs to lean against. This was all the luxury the chiefs had more than the people.

After the sacrifices were offered, betrothment was granted by the high priest. The woman so betrothed did not leave her clan till that day twelve months; but she ranked herself among the married women, learning their customs. On the day of her marriage, she was dressed in the garb of her husband's clan, with the four-cornered napkin or toy, as they called it, upon her head. He then took her for his wife, and land was given him to cultivate for his household. Both his kindred and hers came to assist in the cultivation of his land, and the building of his house. Cattle and all necessary things were given to them by both parties, to help them for the rising generation.

At this time prince Donald the Fifth's wife died in child-bed, with her second child; and in a year after that her oldest son

Donald also died, who was to be ruling prince. There was only one child left, whose name was David; and the prince himself dying shortly afterwards, the whole charge of this child was left upon Laurence the priest, who was the child's uncle; but Laurence appointed one of his nearest kinsmen to be ruler before the child should come of age. So in this way every thing was done in order and in accordance with the laws of the altar—every one doing justly to one another. The child at length arrived at the age of twenty-one years; and the high priest took a lamb, and taking the young man with him, offered it upon the altar in presence of all the congregation. Then the high priest said—"It is not lawful to choose an earthly ruler at the holy altar of God; but we shall go to the top of yonder hill, and he that is for him let him uncover his head and turn to the right, and he that is against him let him keep on his bonnet and turn to the left." This place was afterwards called Bonnet Hill, where all disputes were settled before they ascended the Hill of God, to offer their sacrifices at the holy altar. So all the people took off their bonnets and turned to the right hand, and cried out—"We will have David for our prince, and none other." Then Saint Laurence and the young prince, with all the rulers and elders, went to Montrose; and the near kinsman then gave his charge to the young prince. He was then seated on the Marble Chair, and his feet upon the Stone Pillow, and Laurence said—"I anoint thee, in the name of the Lord, to be prince and ruler over this people; and as thy father was not spared to bless thee, yet the Lord shall bless thee and protect thee, and see that thou rulest justly, and givest to every man according to his family and needs; for the land is the Lord's, and the fulness thereof." Then Saint Laurence took his journey again to Dundee to his own clan; and in about twelve months afterwards the young prince David, was betrothed to the daughter of the chief of the M'Intyre clan, and he took her home at the time appointed.

In the reign of prince David there was nothing of importance that occurred, until his son Donald grew up to manhood. He then came to the altar and offered a lamb for a sin offering for his original sin. It happened on that day that there was a woman of the clan M'Intyre who was betrothed to a young man of the M'Donald clan, and Donald coveted her at the holy altar. He then went to David his father and said—"I pray thee, let me have that young woman who was betrothed to-day." The prince said—"My son, thou hast coveted that which is not thine or mine; thou hast broken the law of the altar, and thou canst not have her; therefore thou must shew works meet for repentance." Instead of repenting, however, he went and consulted a number of young men and took her by force, which grieved his father very much. He then gathered a rival party and rebelled against his father. He was a fierce and furious-looking man, and, from his appearance, was called Donald Grim. Prince David, being grieved in his heart with the conduct of his son, went to Laurence the high priest to get counsel concerning the matter; and the high priest said—"Let us not be like the Gentiles—raise no quarrel and shed no blood, but call all the people together, those that believe in the prophecies and word of God, and come unto me." So David came again to Montrose, and did according as the priest had told him. The people took the Marble Chair and Jacob's Pillow, and came again to the high priest; and he said to David—"Tarry thou with me until I send my young men to find a place for thee and thy people."

So early next morning they they took their departure up the river, on light barges, and came as far as the evening tide carried them. They saw that there was plenty of fish in the river. The mountains were covered with large oaks, and there was also plenty of deer and roebuck in the forest. The land seemed very fertile and beautiful. They then returned and gave in their report concerning the land they had seen. The prince and the high priest were both pleased with the good news; and Laurence took a ram and offered it upon the holy altar, and prayed to the Lord, and commended the prince to the Lord, and all his people. So the prince departed and all his host; but his wife and young family remained with the priest, until her dwelling was prepared. The people floated on the barges up the river till they landed at the place that the young men had told them of, and the prince called the name of the place Port David. They were immediately ordered to build an altar to the Lord. They built it in the usual manner, with twelve stones round the outside circle, representing the twelve tribes of Israel. Laurence the high priest, of Dundee, offered a ram for a peace offering, and a lamb for a sin offering, and called all the clan Donald together, as they were very numerous, and said to them—" See that ye be loyal to the priest and to your rulers, so that the blessing of God may abide among you." Then Laurence the priest and his young men returned home again, and David and his men began to build a synagogue to the Lord. They afterwards built a dwelling for prince David. When all this was accomplished, he brought home his wife and family. She still mourned over her rebellious son; but the priest said—" Do not mourn for him, for the Lord will deal with him as seemeth good in his sight." Donald Grim, as he was called, was debarred, and all his followers, from coming to the altar to offer any kind of sacrifice, neither were they betrothed at the altar to any of the young virgins of either of the clans, but were perfect rebels or outlaws. Time rolled on till Donald Grim was found drowned in the river Es... or the fish river. Then the woman that he coveted at the altar, and the son of Donald Grim came to Dundee to offer a sin offering for his original sin; but old Saint Laurence said—" Not so, you must go and seek the forgivenness of prince David." So the mother and her son came to Port David, and bowed herself before Prince David, and sought forgivenness for herself and her son and all the people. Her father-in-law fully forgave her, and told her to go in the name of the Lord to the high priest, and he would tell her what to do. So she came again to Dundee, to the high priest, and he told her to go home to her own place for seven years and humble herself, and all her people, and her son likewise, and come again at the end of seven years, and if their works were meet for repentance, then they all would be accepted. At the end of seven years, at the high festival, she came again, and her son and all her people, and there met with her father-in-law, prince David, and after being examined by the elders, they were accepted. The high priest then took a lamb, and offered it for the original sin of young Donald Graham or M'Grimmond, as he was now called, and told him all the laws of the altar. Prince David came forward and anointed him prince of Montrose. The young man said to the prince—"What sign shall I shew to my people, to let them know that I am related to thee?" The prince said—"A rampant lion with his tongue out, and a stripe of red for thy father's clan, which are the M'Donalds, and a stripe of blue for thy mother's clan, which are the M'Intyres." So he and all his people departed in peace from the high festival, and came again to Montrose, and reigned as prince there.

At this time, Laurence of Dundee sent one of his grandsons to be priest to the young prince at Montrose. Laurence the high priest seeing that he was an old man and stricken down with age, called his son, who was also named Laurence, and said unto him—"My son, my journey is almost at an end, and I leave the charge of my people with thee; and see that thou shalt walk in the ways of the Lord, as I have taught thee, and deal justly to every one; and see that thou workest with thine own hands, lest thou shouldst become a burden to the people; and live at peace with them, as nothing else shall annoy thee for many years." And the young man said to his father—"I pray thee, grant me the spirit of prophecy, that I may prophecy as my father and forefathers have done, that I may be enabled to answer the people aright when they question me, lest they find me ignorant." And the high priest said—"My son, hast thou been so long with me, and taught by me, and knowest thou not these things? The spirit of prophecy is not mine to give thee; but cast thyself upon the Lord, and tell him thy desire, and offer secret sacrifice upon the altar; and the Lord grant thee thy desire." Shortly afterwards the high priest died and was buried, and the people mourned for him three times seven days. And when the days of mourning were ended, Laurence the Sixth arose and washed and anointed himself, and took a lamb, and called together all the people, and said—"I offer this lamb before the Lord and all the congregation for my original sin. My father is now gone the way of all the earth, and I charge you all to do justly to one another, that you may bring no reproach upon the cause. He reigned only a few years, when a large star appeared in the east, and rolled toward the west, discharging fire from it. The ruler and the people, seeing this, ran to the young prophet to see what it meant. The prophet said—"I will answer this question by high noon to-morrow before all the people." So Laurence, remembering his father's words, took a lamb and offered it upon the altar secretly, and cried in earnest prayer to the Lord, that he might make known to him His will, and make the mystery of this star plain, so that he might be enabled to show it to the people. And in the visions of the night the Lord shewed unto the priest the mystery of the star, and said to him—" The next year is the Sabbath of the land, and the Lord's release. Tell every man to prepare his land, and lay up a double portion of all sorts of provisions, as there is to be no work done during that year, for I am to bring about the purification of the land." On the morrow all the people assembled, and the priest told them the words of the Lord, how that He was to purify the land, and that every man was to till his ground, and prepare for the Sabbath of the land, and lay up a double portion of all sorts of provisions, as there was to be no work done, for the land was to be purified. So it came to pass at the time appointed that there came a severe storm of snow and frost which lasted for three times seventy-seven days, so that all the unclean beasts died—satrass, wild boars, serpents and snakes, black bears, wolves, and all that were not provided for, died in this storm. On the high festival day the priest provided a ram, and offered it upon the altar for the sins of the people, and a lamb for a thanksgiving offering for the Lord's goodness toward them; and he prayed for all the people, and committed them to the Lord's keeping, and said—"See that your hearts lust not, nor covet that which is not thine; stray not from the laws of the Lord, but keep them strictly." He then blessed the people and let them go. The next year was the eighth year of his reign, and he was betrothed to one of the clan M'Donald; the son of Donald Graham was betrothed to Mary M'Laren, a sister of the priest; and Laurence M'Laren, was betrothed to one of the daughters of M'Intyre, the prince of Kinclaven. It will be remembered that the clan M'Intyre were hunted out of Kinclaven by the satrass; but after the purification of the land they returned again.

Again the Lord appeared to the high priest, and said—" Why remainest thou here, while my people come on pilgrimage to thee, and thou goest not on pilgrimage ? Call all the elders and rulers together, and offer sacrifice for thy neglect. It was well for thy fathers to remain here, when the people were small in number; but now they are become a great nation. Thou must go to the top of a hill which I shall show thee, and offer sacrifices there, and all my people shall come thither also; and thou shalt divide the land by lot, as it was told thee before. As thou hast displeased me, and hast not been strict in keeping my laws, thou shalt be seventy-seven days on pilgrimage to this hill ; then shalt thou and all the people return home. All the yearly transactions shall be rectified there, and the young women and the young men shall be betrothed there ; for there shall be my holy altar." He called the name of the hill Ben-Lawers, and the lake and the river he called St. Laurence. The Lord also said to him -" I will bless thee with twelve sons. Thou shalt not let their land beside thine, but shalt send them east, west, north, and south, so that they may be separated and not go together ; for they shall be priests to my people, and thou shalt bring them up in the fear of thy God, and teach them the laws of the altar, so that they may serve me faithfully." After these sons grew up to be young men, they each of them took their departure to their several spheres of duty. The oldest son remained with his father ; the second son crossed the river to the south (they called him James the blythe, as he was a man of a pleasant countenance) ; the third son, Daniel, became priest to the ruler of Port David, now called Forteviot ; the fourth son went to the west of Adamsdale as priest to M'Kay of the Law, now called Duncrub—he preached in the cottar town of St David, now called Dunning, and he was priest to four synagogues between Dunning and Dalukinzie, or weeping haugh, now called Comrie ; the fifth son, Hugh, went from Comrie to Ardonic, and preached down the lake side until he met with his brother Thomas, the sixth son ; Thomas taught down the lake mouth to Kinclaven; the seventh son preached or taught from Kinclaven to St. John's Town, now called Perth ; the eighth son, Michael, taught from St. John's Town to St. Michael's

Kirk, now called Kirkmichael; the tenth son, Robert, taught from his father's altar round the sea coast, meeting with his kinsman at St. Laurencekirk; the eleventh son, Arnelius or Angus, taught towards the western border of Graham's country; and the twelfth son, Peter, taught round the outside borders of M'Intyre's country, till he met with his brother Michael of Kirkmichael. They all agreed to take their lots of land round the outskirts of the congregation where their father had appointed them. Their father also told them that the spirit of prophecy was not to be given them by man; but by secret sacrifice, prayer, and fasting, the Lord would grant it in measure according to their faith. They then said to their father—"By what sign or token shall the people know that we belong to thee?" And he answered them—"On your breast you shall wear the blue and scarlet. The blue denotes the truth and stedfastness of the word, and the scarlet denotes the persecutions the Church must come through. So the blue and scarlet shall be your badge, and ye shall be known by it. When you go to provide venison for your house, your arrow shall have one wicker, so that the deer may be proven. Lest thou take that which belongeth to the people, ye shall also fish for your own use, and labour your own land—this shalt thou do as the Lord thy God giveth thee strength. Whatever presents may be brought to the altar, thou shalt not bring them into thy house, nor take them for thine own use; but thou shalt leave them with the elders and rulers of the congregation, to divide among the poor and needy, the widow and the fatherless. Ye shall choose twelve elders for every synagogue; and when thou shalt go on a journey, the first man that meets thee, if he shall ask thee thou shalt turn in with him, but thou shalt not dwell two nights under his roof; for the covetous man of this world shall come unto thy altar. Go, then, in peace, and nothing shall annoy thee if thou shalt keep the laws of God until the oldest son of Saint Laurence of Dundee be drowned in the river—then the coming of the Messiah is at hand." So their father blessed them, and they all departed—every man to his own place. They lived in peace for many years, the one generation succeeding the other, until they became a very large people.

It happened then on a day that young Saint Laurence of Dundee was crossing the river to visit his friends, that a dreadful storm arose, and he and all those that accompanied him were drowned. At this there arose a great cry among the people, every one running to his priest and rulers, asking the question— "When will the Messiah come? for this, the prophecy of Saint Laurence the Sixth has come to pass." Some of the priests were praying and seeking the spirit of prophecy; but the Lord did not grant it. They began at this time to get very careless in the observance of the laws of God, and they very seldom came to the altar to offer sacrifice, saying in their hearts—"It has been well with us in times gone by, and it will be well with us in times to come, seeing that the Messiah has not come, according to prophecy." Saint Laurence being drowned, the lawful heir of Dundee, a young man, the second son of James, called Laurence, was made priest in the place of his grandfather; for the M'Larens still kept the laws of the altar; so also did the M'Donalds.

It happened on the first day of May, or May Day, that Marjory or May M'Donald, the daughter of Prince Donald of Forteviot, went to the Oak Forest with all her maids, to make their butter and cheese and spin their lint. As there were no wheels in those days, they spun with the rock and spindle. There was a small synagogue built here by the royal party, and the name of the place is called Chapelhaugh, near to the Path of Condie. They resorted thither in the summer season, when the prince and the young men went a hunting. There was also a river close by which they called May's River, after the young lady; for she and her maids washed in it. It is now called the Water of May. One morning to their great surprise, May and her maids saw in the forest a man who shone like the rising sun. The young lady ran to her father in great haste, and said—"Truly, father, I have seen a god this morning." Her father said—"Hold your peace, leud woman." But she still affirmed that she had truly seen a god. He answered her again—"There shall be no god on the earth till the true Messiah shall come; and, according to prophecy, that is not the form he shall come in." So next morning he arose and took his young men with him, and went to the forest, where, to their no small surprise, they saw not a few of the men his daughter had called gods. These were the first of the human race they had seen apart from their own clans, since they landed at Montrose, or Red Head. The prince was very much alarmed, and called together all his priests, rulers, and elders, and said—" What meaneth all these men that I have seen in the forest ?" And the high priest said—" It must be the advance party of an army upon us, as it is prophecied that the announcement of the Messiah shall come with a rude messenger ; for the people have got careless of all the laws of God—they neither offer sacrifice nor support the widow, the fatherless, nor the orphan ; neither do they mind the old and infirm, but go on in their careless manner ; and remember, Laurence the Sixth of Dundee said that when the laws of God were not kept we would fall into many snares and troubles." So the prince consulted all his rulers as to what was to be done ; and after consultation he ordered all the young men to turn out and clear all the oak hills of cattle, and deer, and all goods beyond the swamps, now called St. David's River, or the River Earn. There they remained offering sacrifices to the Lord, and waiting with patience to see what would become of them.

These men whom they had seen in the forest were in reality a despatch from the Roman army ; for when they viewed the country they returned again to Eatonculda, the founder of Edinburgh, who was then building Edinburgh Castle, about thirty-five years before the birth of Christ. This despatch told all they had seen about the country—that it was cultivated and inhabited, and that there was plenty of cattle and deer to be found in it. Eatonculda then despatched a letter to Rome, telling the emperor what they had discovered. Thereupon, the emperor sent Suspacia, a young Roman general, to raise armies from all the nations he had conquered, and to provide wood cleavers, water carriers, horse drivers, tent makers, and slaves for the Roman army. He then made all these nations pay tribute to keep up his army In the first place, Agriculda was ordered to advance a party of his men with flat-bottomed barges. This party, going across the Forth, found the place all deserted of cattle and deer, and no living creature was to be seen. On this adventure they lost almost all their advance men, owing to the inclemency of the weather and starvation; for the M'Donald, M'Laren, M'Kay, and M'Adam clans had all removed to the north, leaving everything bare and desolate. Few of this advance party returned, which fact discouraged Agriculda, and kept back Suspacia from his advance until further orders from the emperor. Ultimately, a Roman named Loachdoach was despatched with a company of slaves to cut down trees, make roads, build bridges, and make fortresses. This company, arriving at Edinburgh, went up the south side of the Forth, and came to a place called Turnlin, where the tide turned. Here Loachdoach and his party began to build a fortress, and called it Snowton, which fortress was founded about twenty-five years before the birth of Christ. This place is now called Stirling. There he and all his army had to winter. They made themselves clay huts to live in; but owing to a heavy fall of snow upon the flat roofs of the huts (they being built in the eastern fashion) they mostly all fell in upon them, burying them in the ruins. With the exception of some ancient Britons who had been enslaved, nearly all the Roman army perished in this way, from the falling in of their huts, and the inclemency of the weather. Loachdoach, at this time, gathered together the few that remained and went to Edinburgh to consult Agriculda; and it was settled by the emperor's orders that they were to advance again, with all the masons and craftsmen that could be spared, in order to build a safe fortress for the troops. This fortress is now called Stirling Castle. At the south of Stirling they discovered lime, and began the burning of it, and used it as mortar. Anything they had in the way of cement they brought with them; but after this discovery of lime there was less of the cement used. They soon finished all their masonry work, and the recruited army marched to Stirling as their head-quarters in the spring of the year. They then began to build a bridge of timber across the Forth, which bridge was planned by Loachdoach. They contended with the water for several years; and no sooner had they built it than it was swept away. They, however, succeeding in getting Suspacia's party across, and encamped at Ardoch. This Suspacia was the founder of the Ardoch Camps, and he was the father of Titus, the Roman emperor. Suspacia viewed that part of the country, and found that all the people were fled except a few helpless women and children. He also found that there were no provisions of any sort, for the land had not been laboured nor the fields sown the year previous, and they were left to utter starvation—there being no deer and cattle but a few belonging to those poor women who were taken by the Romans. The best and fairest of women were taken by the Romans. Many of them ran to the house of God, expecting to find shelter, but they were torn away; for the Romans valued not the house of God, nor their cry of pity, but used every one according as they thought proper. At this time the winter came on, and there was no provision for the camps. One Bleania, another general of the Roman army, was despatched with a party of slaves and soldiers to make an attack upon the Grampian Mountains, where it was supposed the clans had fled to. The place now called Dunblane derived its name from this Roman general. He took possession of St. David's synagogue for his quarters. At this time, or shortly afterwards, all the synagogues were destroyed by the Romans, except one back in a moor near Longside, at a place called Battlehouse. A great many women were concealed there, and they could not find them out. This place cannot now be found, neither any trace of it. The Romans at this time joined together; but the winter closed in upon them so severe that they were not able to stand it, nor come out of their couches. Excepting the Gulfs and Vandulfs (two northern nations the Romans had conquered), a few Picts, Scots, and Britons, whom they had enslaved, were all that stood the campaign. They settled to cross St. David's River when it was frozen, to attack the people supposed to be on the Grampian Mountains; but by the time the river was frozen the men were unable to be removed, and the females whom they had captured made their escape across the river to their friends. The Romans remained in this position all the winter, and when the storm broke up they were not strong enough for an attack upon the Grampian Mountain savages, as they called them. The two Roman generals, Suspacia and Bleania, were forced to fall back to Dunblane, and were there supported from the head-quarters at Stirling Castle. They had to remain in this position until they reported their circumstances to Claudia, the Roman emperor. The orders of the emperor, on receiving their report, was to send his own fleet to the west of the Grampian Mountains, to a river called Claudia, after his own name; but now called Clyde. There they built a fortress called Briton's Hill, now called Dumbarton. In this fortress they wintered, finding the same hardships and difficulties as the other armies; and early in the spring Claudia returned again to Italy, leaving the charge of his army in the hands of two Roman generals, Leania and Whidarria, brothers, who got orders to join the remainder of Suspacia and Bleania's armies. A great many slaves were sent by Loachdoach to make a road to Dumbarton, in order to join the armies together; for Leania and Whidarria could not join the armies, although within twelve miles of them, and they were forced to remain at Leany, now called Callander. They placed Britons through that part of the country, and called the place Bowes of Whidarria, now called Balquhidder. There they remained all the winter, and few of the Britons went back to the Camp of Callander; but early in the spring of the year all the armies joined at Dunblane—the three kings, King Anglo, the King of High Barony, and the King of Scotia, heading each his army. Suspacia being field-marshal, returned again to Ardoch Camps with his whole army.

Prince Donald who was at Ben Lawers, near Comrie, had meanwhile sent out spies, who returned and told him that the Romans were rapidly advancing towards Ardoch. Women and men whom they had captured as slaves were offered their lives and great rewards if they would lead their army across the passes at St. David's River; but they refused to do so, and said they would rather suffer death before they would betray their country. Many men and women, therefore, were put to death in a most cruel manner for the fidelity they bore to their country. By this time all the Roman army had got settled at Ardoch Camps, and had provided houses for their wives and families. Loachdoach's party, who were all slaves, began to cut a road from the woods to to the north-west, in order to cross at the top of the swamp; and in a few days they arrived at St. David's River, near the seat of Saint Laurence.

The report reached Saint Laurence that the Romans were at hand; and the rulers, elders, and saints consulted what was to be done. Saint Laurence said—" From the earliest prophecy we have had by Lazarus the First, we believe this is the land that the Lord hath provided for us, and generations after us yet to come. It is true we have had to fly from Carthagena, leaving part of the people behind us; we had to fly from Troy East, leaving some behind us; and had also to fly from Gaul, leaving many behind us there that fled to the wilderness. The chief ruler's blood stained the shore before ever the foot of man trod it; and truly this must be the land the Lord hath promised to us and our seed after us. Therefore, fast and pray for three successive days, and uncover your heads and your feet, so that they may be wet with the dews of heaven; and go to a high mountain, and there pour forth your lament, and cry to the Lord." This hill, or mountain, is near Comrie, and is now called the Weeping Mount. Early on the morning of the third day, after he had received the report, Saint Laurence arose and repaired the altar, and offered a lamb for a sin offering and a ram for a peace offering; after which he called together all the elders and saints of each congregation, and ordered them to take their people and walk round the hill, and cry to the Lord for deliverance. He then went to the altar and covered himself with sackcloth and ashes, and prayed to the Lord to grant him the spirit of prophecy; but the Lord did not grant it, but caused a deep sleep to fall upon him, and in his sleep there appeared unto him, standing upon the corner stone of the altar, a man clothed in a long white robe, with a two edged sword, and a crown on his head which shown like the brightness of the sun; and he said to Saint Laurence—" Arise, and shake off thy fears; for God hath heard thy cries and weeping, and hath promised to be with thee, and he shall visit that place with terrible things, as the first fruits of his vine shall fall there; but he that continueth to the end shall receive the crown of life." So Saint Laurence arose early on the fourth morning, and called with a loud voice for all the congregations to come near to the altar; and he spoke to the people, and said—" String your bows and prepare for battle, for the Lord hath said He shall give thee victory over all thy foes." At this, the people all spoke out and said—" We are not prepared with our armour and horses so as to meet our enemies." The saint thus answered them—" Believe what the Lord hath said, and doubt not; for he that doubteth shall be cut off from among the people." While yet the saint was speaking, a messenger came with the sad tidings that the Romans had broken into the synagogue of the Mourning Haugh, and had taken all the fair women and virgins who were placed there for safety, destroying all the synagogue of the Lord. At this sad news Saint Laurence said to the people—" Seeing that the Lord hath promised to be shield spear, and helmet to you, why do you fear to go forward?" They then hastily prepared themselves and began to move forward. The clan M'Grimmond, now called Graham, got their badge (the rampant lion with his tongue hanging out), and were sent to guard the Freeton Pass, now called Crieff. The badge of the clan M'Intyre was a ship, as their name was derived from their trade; this clan went to guard Strome Pass, now called Strowan. They were ordered to keep the passes strictly, and to let no one pass, lest the Romans might close in between them and the mountains. M'Grimmond, the leader, told his men to take off their plaids and make tents for their women, children, and old men. The place of this occurence was called Plaided Field, now called Inchbrakie. All the passes were secured by the orders of Prince Donald. M'Kay, the Prince of the Law, now called Duncrub, was highly offended at Graham getting the badge of the lion. The saint, however, went to him and told him not to be offended at his brother, for he would be allowed to have any beast in the field as his badge. He then chose as his badge the mountain cat, one of the fiercest animals in existence. This was the foundation of the clan Cattan, which was a fierce and warlike band.

In course of time the Romans advanced to the edge of the river, and putting the women and virgins they had captured in the synagogue in the front of the army, they offered them to their friends, if they would only surrender to them and pay them homage; but Prince Donald and all the rulers and elders boldly declared that they would not surrender. At this time a dispute arose in the Roman army about the captured women; some were for slaying them in front of the battle before their friends, some were for them to fall behind the army, while others bore respect and love to them, and would have dealt more kindly with them. At the same time, while this dispute was going on, the Cattans and Ruthvens were engaged on the left, in which engagement a heavy loss befel the Romans. On hearing of this, Suspacia ordered the whole army to press forward, sparing neither women nor children; for it was the first time the Roman flag had been insulted. The battle raged furiously for some time; but the Romans were ultimately driven back and defeated. The youngest son of M'Kay headed a band of bowmen and kept the broken grounds, the rocks, and the woods, tormenting the Romans very much, and often closing in upon them unawares. The M'Donalds and M'Larens had now crossed the river, and were fighting hand to hand with the Romans, who had by this time suffered severely from the arrows of their enemies. Feeling that they were about to experience a second defeat, and the Romans cried—" Curse that field of pins," the mountaineer bowmen having punished them severely with their arrows, which they called pins. This place is now called Dalganross. The M'Donalds and M'Larens kept shoulder to shoulder in the midst of the battle, and so strongly and successfully opposed the Romans that they came off with heavy losses. The Cattans and Ruthvens caused much havoc in the rear of the Roman army, they being very expert bowmen. The battle raged so furiously that they were at last fighting hand to hand. Every attack of the Romans, however, was repulsed with heavy losses. While the Cattans were engaged firing at the Romans they killed many of the M'Larens; but immediately the Cattans and Ruthvens put shoulder to shoulder in order to stem the red stream, and catching spears and swords where they could find them, they attacked the Roman army on the left wing, and drove them into great confusion. In this cruel attack fell St Laurence of Lawers, and the ruler, prince Donald of Fort David. John, the youngest son of Saint Laurence, unmindful of his affectionate father's death, cried—" Hold at her (meaning the goddess Mermaid, the standard of the Roman army); forward to death or victory!" This John, son of Saint Laurence, was the founder of clan Comrie, now Montgomery. The fearful battle was closed with the darkness of night.

Early next morning, all the clans having again joined together, they found that the Romans had exercised their brutal revenge on the helpless women and men whom they had captured and made slaves, and who belonged to the clans. Their cruelty was most revolting; for they even went as far as opening them up and letting their bowels fall out, and even compelling them afterwards till exhaustion and death put an end to their sufferings. All this cruelty was executed by their Gorrier, so called because he cut up the people alive. They had also one they called the Skinner, who skinned the people alive, and another they called the Pinner, who pinned them to death. These three monsters were always along with the Roman camp. The place where these cruelties were perpetrated was called Dalrannoch, or Roaring Haugh; while the place where their mangled bodies were buried was called Catherine's Haugh, or Dalkettle. The young men were sent back to the field where the battle was fought the day before to gather all the arrows they could find from among the dead and wounded, as their arrows were all spent. The youngest son of M'Kay, who was called Neish, slipped stealthily along among the bushes to discover if possible what the Romans were about, and soon saw them offering sacrifice to Fortune, and that with the fairest young women whom they had captured. On seeing this, he immediately repaired to the rulers of the clans, and laid his report before them. Young Saint Laurence, now in his eighteenth year, erected a temporary altar, and offered thereon a lamb for his original sin, a ram for a thanksgiving offering, and a goat for a success offering for the day;

and all the rulers and elders of the congregation engaged in prayer with the young saint.

At this time the Romans, thinking that the clans could advance no further, came down the hill with great fury, calling on all the gods of Rome to assist them. When the word came to the clans from the outside watchmen that the Romans were advancing, every chief, taking command of his own clan, advanced, crying— "The God of Bethel be with us." Immediately on the Romans advancing within bowshot, the clans, with sure and steady aim discharged their arrows upon them, and they fell in hundreds. The Romans, when they saw that the clans were not shaken in their courage, ran back and fled towards Ardoch, and drew themselves up in battle order, cursing the Gods of Rome for their failure. This place was called Blairnroar, or the Roaring Battle. The clans immediately pursued, keeping their bowmen in the rear of the Roman army, and making great havoc. The chief of the M'Kays, remembering that there was a synagogue at the back of the hill from Longside, and being anxious as to its safety, extended his lines on the south side of the swamp, holding the Romans in the soft and marshy ground. This battle being fought by the bowmen, the clans that day made no charge upon their enemy; for they had seen that arrows were scarce with the Romans.

The clouds now began to gather and darken all along the western sky, while the rain fell in torrents, streaming down the hills, and forcing the two armies to withdraw. The rain beat so vehemently in the face of the Roman army that they had to take shelter on the east side of the river, while the clans went to the south-west. The two armies lay within sight of each other for three days, but no fighting took place between them. M'Kay of the Law, who took the place of M'Donald, who was slain in the field, sent a despatch to the M'Intyres and Grahams, ordering them to leave the passes and join them immediately, as he knew not at what moment the enemy might attack them. Finding, however, that the banks of St. David's River were all overflown with the torrents of rain, and all the swamps impassable, he immediately sent another despatch for John Roy, the brother of Saint Laurence, who was distinguished from the rest of his brothers by his hair being red. From this man sprang the Roys in the Lowlands, and the M'Roys in the Highlands. He was a mountain forester, and followed the camp with cattle. On receiving the despatch he at once got his men in readiness and advanced to join the clans; and as they were all expert bowmen they added very much to the strength of the army.

On the fourth day after the storm above narrated, the Romans turned out all the slaves and camp followers, cleavers of wood and carriers of water, and put them in ranks between the two armies, to enable their army to get in upon the clans. The clans, however, fell back, and would not fall upon unarmed men; for the slaves had no weapons except their axes, picks, and such tools as they laboured with. Seeing that the river and swamps were now passable, M'Kay sent another despatch to the M'Intyres and Grahams, ordering them to come round by Red Field, in order to gather all the swords, spears, and arrows they could possibly find, so that they might be prepared to join the clans in another attack against the Romans.

Next morning a great many slaves fled from the Roman camp to the camp of the clans, where they were sure to meet with a friendly reception. They had in fact fled to the protection of those who in reality were their own kinsmen; for it was their forefathers who were captured from among the Hebrews when they were in Gaul. They were admitted into the camp of the clans, and there they gave the whole details of the Roman proceedings, and the strength of their army, and stated that the women and children and most of the leaders had fled all together to a camp they previously made at a place called Leania, now called Callander; but still the Roman army was in a good condition. Soon, however, was heard the sound of the pibroch, accompanied by a fierce and warlike band. This was the M'Intyres and Grahams, another strong addition to the army of the clans. The clans all joined together in offering sacrifice and in prayer; and the hearts of these poor captives who had just joined them bounded with joy and gratitude when they were at liberty to worship and praise the God of Bethel, who at last had delivered them out of that slavery and bondage in which they had been held since their forefathers had parted from them. Here they all broke up again in clans—every leader with his own clan. James the Ruthven led the M'Larens; the prince of Kinclaven, M'Intyre, led the M'Intyres; the prince of Montrose led the M'Grimmonds or Grahams; M'Kay of the Law led the Cattans, the M'Donalds, the M'Kays, and the Neishes. These last four clans were very few in number, as they nearly all fell in the field.

At this time the enemy, seeing the proceedings of the clans, and the desertion of their slaves, became quite disheartened, and made their retreat. Graham and M'Intyre went to the head ruler, M'Kay of the Law, and asked him to withdraw the clans that had been so much cut up, and they would give the Romans a hearty welcome. Ardoch Camp at this time was wholly deserted by the Romans, their whole force being in the field. The M'Intyres and Grahams being in good heart, and determined to avenge the blood of their kinsmen, kept their bowmen close on the rear of the Roman army. Arthur and Alpine were very useful in collecting the arrows of the clans. The Romans turned on the clans at Bleania's Hill, now Dunblane; but John Roy and his son and party had been sent by James the Ruthven, chief of the M'Larens, to watch the proceedings of the Romans; and instead of going back to give tidings of their proceedure, they successfully, because unexpectedly, fell upon the left wing of the Roman army, forcing them to quit the field, cursing the gods of Rome.

Some more of the captives had now deserted from the Romans, bringing with them the tidings that Loachdoach, one of the Roman generals, was about to build a wooden bridge near Craigforth for the retreat of the army. Loachdoach's party were never heard of afterwards; and when the retreating army came to the place where they expected to find the bridge, it was only to be disappointed; for the heavy waters had again swept it away. They were thus forced to go round by Gartmore.

The season was now far advanced, and owing to exposure to the cold, many of the Romans died. The Roman leader, Suspacia, now sought to make an agreement with the clans that he would deliver up all the worshippers of the God of Bethel, or the Unknown God, and that he would not trouble them for a generation to come, if they would allow him and his army quietly to retire. A message was sent by M'Intyre and Graham to the chief rulers, M'Kay and James Ruthven, to see if they would settle on these conditions. The conditions were accepted, and Suspacia at once came forward with all the captives who wished to leave the Romans. The head or chief among these captives was one called Saint Lennox, who was a priest of the altar before captured by the Romans. Great was the joy of these people when they joined their brethren. Saint Lennox became a priest and ruler of his people at Britain's Hill, now called Dumbarton Castle.

The Romans then took their departure, but instead of going home to their own country they went to that which was afterwards the country of the ancient Britons and Scots—nations founded by the Romans, and that paid tribute to them.

After this heavy and bloody struggle, the Caledonians fell back into their mountains. They married and were given in marriage, and their customs remained the same. Margaret, the daughter of Saint Laurence of Lawers, was married to Saint Lennox of Dumbarton. She had two sons who went under the same designation. One of these went to the south with a party. He got a grant of land from the rulers. They called the place Saint Lennox; it is now called Lanark. This place was founded as a place of defence against the Scots or any other enemy that might attack them, and the River Clyde was granted to them for a fishing river. The other brother got a grant of land from the rulers at Lennox Forest, now Lyndoch. This saint was married to one of the M'Intyres of Kinclaven. Saint Alpin, married Mary M'Donald, the daughter of the high ruler M'Donald, who fell in the field. He got a grant of land which was called Doon Alpin, now called Duplin. This Alpin acted as regent for the young Prince Donald, as he was only about eight years of age. He was also the first of the M'Alpine or M'Gregor race. James the son of Arthur of Glenerton, was called James the Waldense, to distinguish him from the rest of the clans.

He married Helen, the daughter of M'Kay of the Law, and got a grant of land. In the troublous times the name was changed to Halden or Halley or Hall. They were numbered among the martyrs. The son of Saint Lennox of Dumbarton, who was also a slave under the Roman yoke, was married to Elizabeth, daughter of the Graham who pursued the Romans. He succeeded his father as priest and ruler at Dumbarton. The son of M'Kay of the Law got a grant of land which was called the Forest, and is now called Auchterarder; and there he built a castle which was a long time a royal residence; and on the west of this castle was built an altar, and five stones were placed round it, as there were five tribes who came to worship there. Neish, the youngest son of M'Kay of the Law, was granted Tirlumhill, now called Drummond Castle. His land extended to the water of Macnie, and he was the founder of the clan M'Nish or Nish. Young Saint Lars of Lars succeeded his father, and James Riven got Saint Laurence Plains, his father's residence. James the Blyth and his race returned back to Clutcher Rock, or Clan Claren Rock. He was the first of the Blythes of Fife. This Blyth was one of the clan M'Laren, but derived his name from his countenance being pleasant and fair to look upon. John, the youngest son of Saint Lars, got his land at a spot called Comrie. By this time the Caledonians were all settled down, and living in peace and quiet. Building was going on, and fortifications were built in every place where it was thought necessary, the Law among other places, M'Kay's residence near Duncrub; and a palace was built on the north side of the swamp, now called Gaskhall. This was a place of safety for the royal party who lived at Port David. The oldest son of Graham of Montrose returned with his father. The second son was ruler at Gartmore, as a barrier to any approaching enemy. The third son got a grant of land from Freeton, now called Crieff, down to the land of M'Alpin, now Duplin. All these chiefs were as rulers to see the land justly divided among the people, and faithful stewards to their Heavenly Master. Arthur the Waldense and Evans were considered to be of the clan of Daniel or M'Donald; the other two, Alpine and Lennox were considered to be of the clan Laurence or M'Laren. They were descendants of those who believed not in the prophecy of Lazarus the First, but afterwards repented, and worshipped the God of Bethel. Many of the race of Saint Laurence were priests at the early age of eighteen, owing to so many of the saints being slain in the field. The clans were dreadfully cut up, leaving many a widow and fatherless child. The son of James the Blyth, called Nathaniel, by the assistance of the Waldenses, built Castle Law, a place of strong defence, once called Nathaniel's Land, but now Abernethy. His land joined with the royal forest. The march was the Rocking Stone which was placed by some of the Waldenses; it also joined with his father's land on the other side. John Mealon afterwards Melville, dwelt Athwart the Muir, now called Milnathort. He was one of the royal princes of Forteviot or Port David. He was joined by a part of every clan, as he dwelt on the southmost border, and was in jeopardy of being attacked by the enemy from the south. John Melville built a castle on an island situated in a lake called Loch Leven. He was assisted in this undertaking by the Waldenses, who were expert craftsmen in the arts of building.

The people for the space of sixty years lived in peace and harmony, nothing annoying them. The whole history of the Romans was given by the Waldenses, when they escaped from the Roman camp. They also brought with them the art of building fortifications, and the customs of placing kings, and founding nations.

Anglo, Highburnia, Wales, and Scotta, were four sisters who were married to four kings, according to the wish of the Emperor of Rome, who then named the nations after these sisters. The oldest daughter Scotta was married to the king of Athens' son; she and her husband were the founders of the Scottish nation. Her son, who was named Pharaoh or Fergus, went out to the Holy Land with a party of Scotsmen to fight against the Jews, and it is said that this party were eye-witnesses to the crucifixion of Christ. This Fergus was presented with a small crown by the Roman Emperor; and when the war was over, and they had returned home, Fergus was crowned first king of Scotland. After they conquered the Jews and got all matters settled, Titus being in full power as Emperor of Rome, remembered the words of his father to be avenged of the Great Mountain savages, meaning the Caledonians. He then gave orders that a part of every nation was to be gathered together to destroy them, as he promised to his father. This collection was named the Roman Legion. There were eight leaders, four of whom with their men were to go to the River Claudia, now Clyde, and the other four were to go to the Forth. The orders given them were to lay waste the country with fire and sword, and deliver the fair women up to the troops, or sell them as slaves. Some young men were also to be to be sent to Rome, to be sold as slaves. This soon broke the peace of the Caledonians, and threw them into great trouble.

By this time the Romans had entered into St. Blyth's Land, now called Fife, laying the country waste with fire and sword. As they came along they destroyed almost all the M'Larens of Clatcherd and Abernethy, while those who were spared fled westward to the M'Donalds at Port David. The Romans forced their way forward and encamped at Ardargie. All the clans at this time were summoned to meet upon the Law, near Duncrub, to take council for future steps, and it was there agreed to attack the Romans in order to prevent them from destroying the royal palace at Port David; but when they essayed to do this, the Romans were so numerous that they surrounded the clans, and compelled them to surrender. The two sons of Prince Donald of Port David, Donald and David; the three sons of M'Kay of the Law, James, David, and Donald; two sons of Saint Laurence of Dundee, James and Laurence; these were all taken prisoners in this engagement. The chief of the Grahams, at Graham's Land, now called Gash, was slain in the field; and many more men of value and worth fell at this same battle of Ardargie. The clans were all scattered before the Romans. Adam of Adamsdale was slain and his son taken prisoner. The Lennoxes of Lanark were driven back into the Lands of Graham of Gartmore. The Grahams fled back to the hill called Ben Ledi, where the holy altar stood. The clans of the western district all met there and fortified themselves on the face of the hill.

The Romans encamped again in Callander. The M'Inroys, a branch of M'Larens, kept the pass at Leania. The Romans made an attempt to enter Balquhidder by the mountain pass, and encamped at Ben Voirlich. They were very anxious to get possession of that part of the country, as Whidarria had found gold in several places during the first invasion. The report by this time reached James Ruthven, who had fled to Balquhidder for safety, that the Romans had encamped at Ben Voirlich. At this time the clans were in two divisions, one half of them going with James Ruthven, and the other half remaining to keep the pass at Leania. The M'Inroys led the van, as they were best acquainted with the mountain passes. Next morning, by the break of day, the clans cut the Roman army into two divisions, the one half going down the Lake side, and the other half making the best of their way to Callander, by Glenample; and James the Ruthven slew the last Roman of the party he pursued at Horse Mount, at the head of Glenample. Durn, a Roman general, made the best of his way down the Lake side, and the last of his party sheltered themselves in a place called Dundirn. John Comrie, the son of Comrie, who was so brave during the first invasion, fell upon Durn single-handed, and slew the Roman general on the spot. He then mounted his horse, and carried off his spear. The crest of the Comries or Montgomeries is a man dressed in Durn's armour on horseback, with a spear in his hand. At this time the M'Inroys, who were leading the van, heard the sound of the Roman horn, when James the Ruthven ordered them to lie down among the heather. The Romans having captured one of the Caledonians, thought to be one of the M'Arthurs of Glenarton, he was chained in front of the Roman army, they forcing him to lead the way. At this time John Roy and his bowmen were ordered to attack the flank of the Roman army, and they approached the Romans within bowshot before they were observed; and at the same time James the Ruthven extended his whole line in front of the army. By this time the clans were all armed with the Roman arms they had gathered the day before on the field of battle. They then advanced towards the Romans till within bowshot, and discharged their arrows upon them. John Roy and his party from the sides of the hill attacked them at the same time with their arrows, and made a dreadful slaughter. Comrie with his spearsmen engaged in front of them on the left wing, and James the Ruthven attacked them on the right wing. Brackland, the Roman general, tried to make a retreat, but they were so closed in with the Grahams and Neishes, who had fled from the field of Ardargie, that it was impossible for him to turn to the right hand or to the left, and he and all his party were slain at the Wild Bridge or Bridge of Brackland. This battle was fought on the braes of Leania. Cleshee, one of the Roman generals seeing he was surrounded on every side with kilted clansmen, tried to make his escape with his army, and forded the clear water, now called Cleshee's Ford, to endeavour to join the main army in the east. A party of the Lennoxes, who were lying in ambush, on observing this immediately attacked them by bowmen, but the Lennoxes being so few in number had to fall back to the fortified camps at Ben Ledi, leaving the Romans masters of this part of the field. The chief of the Lennoxes fell that day.. They now call that place Lanark. Cleshee and his men made the best of their way to Bleania Hill Camp, now Dunblane, as this place was a fortified camp of the Romans during the first invasion. From there they marched to Ardoch Camp, called the Romans' Home. There the Roman generals met in council—namely Rossinia, Cardin, Athellia, and Cleshee, the king of that district now called Fife, where he had established a slave market. This king sent a despatch that the Romans were to lie in ambush until he could forward another force to their assistance. Immediately the king sent messengers to Anglo-Wales, which is now called Ancient Britain, Highburnia, now Ireland, and Scota, and also the country now called Denmark. All these nations paid tribute to this king, and had to turn out all their fighting men, or the taxes were doubled that year. All these legions were got forward by the spring of the year, and joined the Roman camp at Ardoch, and immediately orders were given by the Roman generals to march to the plains of Blairdarg, now called Comrie. The clans were then collected at Lars, near Comrie, to take council how they were to come to terms with the Romans, but the Romans would accept of no conditions whatever, but wished the clans to deliver themselves up, either to make slaves of them, or use them for whatever purpose they pleased, as well as their country, for the damage done to the Roman Empire during the last war; but to these conditions the clans would not submit. The Romans then got orders to ford the river and attack the clans on the opposite side. The clans seeing the great number of horsemen and chariots of war, fled to the mountains with considerable loss, and several of them were taken as prisoners. The Romans then ranged over Graham's country, and destroyed everything by fire and sword, until they came to St. Laurence River, now called the Tay. The clans at this time were scattered in broken bands, and all the low plains that had been cultivated were taken by the Romans, who held and occupied the country as far as the river Derm, now called Dee. All the prisoners who were captured in the battles were sent and sold as slaves at the market at a place now called Cupar-Fife, and amongst these slaves were many a prince's son and daughter. Mary M'Donald, the prince's daughter, of Port David, was one of this unhappy band. There were also two of her brothers taken prisoners at the battle of Ardargie. The two sons of St. Lawrence of Dundee were also taken at the same battle, and three sons of M'Kay of the Law. Adam of Adamsdale was also slain, and his son taken prisoner. These nobles were sent off to Rome to be sold at the slave market there. The two sons of M'Donald, the prince, were sold to a man who worshipped the god of Annan. This was the god of the shepherds, and the figure was branded on each breast. The two brothers, M'Kay of the Law, were sold to a man who worshipped Vulcan, the god of fire; and the third son of M'Kay was believed to have died on being sold in Fife as a slave. The two sons of Laurence of Dundee and the son of Adam of Adamsdale were sold to a man who worshipped Bacchus, the god of wine. They were made gardeners and wine pressers. The practice in Rome was that every slave was branded with a figure of the god his master worshipped. No report was ever heard of their brothers or sisters or any of their kindred. At this time the Romans tortured all who were found to worship the Nazarene prophet. The custom of

Rome was that every man who offered sacrifice carried his god about with him. There were days of festival to their gods, and every day of the week the fire of the altar burned, but none of the slaves were allowed to offer their sacrifice till ten years rolled over them. Under this dreadful bondage, with no prospect of escape, the followers of the Nazarene prophet were increasing in number, but the Romans increased their torture to a fearful extent. Some were skinned alive; others were put into cages that contained numbers of eagles of the largest size, to be torn and eaten by them; and others were torn asunder by four horses. But the more they were tortured the more their number increased. Some were put into cauldrons of boiling oil, crying to Jesus of Nazareth to receive their spirit, while the Romans stopped their ears with their fingers, crying out—"Ha, ha! they blasphemed our gods, but their gods hear them not." Others of their tortures were these:—The gorrier opened their bellies, letting their bowels fall out; others were put into a dungeon, and the pinner threw at certain times of the day burning sulphur on them, and ended their days in that dreadful manner. But in their greatest agony they cried the more to Jesus of Nazareth, which was a torture to the Romans, to hear them call upon their Saviour. The number of believers increased so much that they gathered them in old houses and suffocated them with brimstone. They also put them into lions' dens to feed their lions, and they also allowed any one to take the flesh of those martyrs to feed their dogs, or any other use they might think proper, as they gave them no burial. Titus had given orders to all his rulers, that wherever those worshippers were found they were to put them to death in whatever manner they pleased. The rulers of the Temple at Jerusalem told the Roman Governor that if they did not keep down the worshippers of Jesus, and compel the people of Judea and all the country round about to come and offer sacrifice and also pay tribute, that they, the Jews, would not pay tribute to Titus. At this time some of the Roman soldiers turned Christians, which enraged the Jews very much, and they charged the Governor with being partial to the Christians. So far went their jealousy that they ordered the Roman Governor with all his soldiers to leave the city. They then shut the gate against all Roman power, and would no longer pay tribute. Titus hearing all this, his anger was kindled against Jerusalem, and he gave orders to all his captains and commanders, and all his men of war, to get ready to besiege Jerusalem. All the smiths were to follow the army, to make and repair engines for throwing stones against the walls on purpose to break them down; and all those who were branded, and who had been some time in Rome, were ordered to be sent with the army to be cleavers of wood and carriers of water. Amongst those slaves were the sons of Prince Donald of Port David, the sons of M'Kay of the Law, the two sons of Saint Clare of Dundee, and the son of Adam of Adamsdale. All the slaves were served out with a knapsack of camel's skin, hatchets, and mattocks; and during the siege the slaves were brought up to work the engines. David, the son of the prince of Port David, was slain with a stone from the wall. The son of Laurence of Dundee got his leg broken, and his brother James carried him back and laid him down some distance from the city, and then returned to his engine. This siege went on for a long time. The sons of M'Kay of the Law were smiths, and wrought at some distance from the city, and the son of Adam of Adamsdale was a servant in the camp. Donald, the son of the prince of Port David, and James M'Laren, the son of Saint Clare of Dundee, were engaged at their engine at the Sheep Gate. James M'Laren then went in the evening to see if he could find his brother Laurence where he had laid him with his broken leg, and took some food with him, which was very scarce. As slaves were getting no attention from the doctors of the army, he found his brother in great agony, and passed the most of the night with him; but owing to loss of blood and hunger, he died about cock-crowing. So James, after seeing that his brother was dead, returned to his post at his engine, and wrought all day with his heart full of grief. At evening he left his neighbour Donald at his post, and took his spade and dug a grave, near the garden of Gethsemane, and buried his brother. Returning in the dark of night, he saw a light a small distance from him. Thinking it might be a case of distress similar to his own, he drew near to the light, but heard nothing. He drew nearer till he found in a small hole a large number of diamonds set in gold in the form of a crown. He then lifted it and put it in his knapsack, and returned to the sepulchre of his brother, and dug a hole at his feet and buried it, not knowing what it was. He then returned to his companion, and with grief for his dear brother thought little of the article he had placed at his feet. The siege was so long, and they were so hard wrought, and had often so little food, their life became bitter to them. They were often scalded with boiling grease thrown over the walls; but at length a breach was made, and the Romans rushed forward, putting men, women, and children to death, with fire and sword. The sufferings of the Jews at this time were very great. The Romans would make a Jew work at tearing down the Temple, till he would fall down from hunger, and to amuse themselves they would thrust them through with a sword, and pitch them over the walls to be eaten by dogs. They levelled down the whole city so that one could not discern if ever there had been a city there. Whatever a Roman did to a Jew was never called into question. The rulers, priests, and slaves all suffered the same torture, as there was as little respect for the one as the other. By this time the city was in total ruin, and the Romans were always expecting to find some hidden treasure, but very little of that was discovered. The whole country was then visited with a famine and many people died daily.

At this time the Lord visited the Romans specially for the cruelty done to his people. The Roman Emperor having sent orders that no slaves were to be returned to Rome, they were turned out of the camp. All those slaves who spoke the Latin language, as they were considered Romans, and many of the rulers and people of high learning, together with their sons and daughters, were sold among them as slaves in order to preserve their lives, as they were slaying all the Jews by the sword. A Roman merchant in the slave trade bought all the Latin slaves, but would not buy any of the Jewish rebels, as they were called, nor the worshippers of the Nazarene prophet, nor those who adhered to the new laws. As Noustinous, the slave master, would not buy any of these Christian slaves, the Romans burned three holes in their tongues, and then let them go where they pleased. By this time the bought slaves were out of the camp and under their slave master, but he seemed to have more confidence in the branded slaves than in the others, and he gave them the charge of the others. James M'Laren and Donald M'Donald had charge of a number of the slaves, and James leaving his charge for a time went for a parting visit to his brother's sepulchre. While there, he remembered the article he had buried, and then dug it up. Knowing by this time it was something of value, he placed it in his knapsack, and took his journey again to his post. All this time M'Donald knew nothing of his brother David, and considered he had fallen under the ruins of the wall; but next day while on the march he found that the two sons of M'Kay of the Law had been sold along with them, and also the son of Adam of Adamsdale, and they greatly rejoiced when they found they were all in one band, as they had not seen each other during the time of the siege of Jerusalem. They then took shipping, intending to sail for Rome, but when near the landing port a despatch was sent out telling them that no slaves were to be allowed to land, as famine had spread over all the country. The Lord permitted the Romans to persecute the Jews, but he afflicted the Romans with famine and pestilence. As the orders were that no slaves were to be allowed to land there, but were permitted to land either in Britain or Gaul, or Jeremy's Land, or any other port beyond the great god Gib's Rock (the God of the Storm), they set sail from Rome, bound for Jeremy's Land, but a great storm arose, and as one of the slaves named Murdoch cried out—"Oh, Jesus of Nazareth, have mercy on us!" a Roman soldier who had been standing by, overheard him and went and told the shipmaster that there was a slave praying to Jesus, and not to Gib, the god of the storm. Immediately orders were given that he should be hanged and cast overboard, and this was done in presence of his two daughters, Elizabeth and Dightus. Many also of the old men who were infirm were thrown overboard, as their provisions were getting scarce; but the Romans said—"It was on account of these Christians that Jerusalem was destroyed, and are we to lose our lives also?" But still the worshippers of Christ spoke to each other in a quiet way. Saints Canaan and

Chaldea were chained together, and had communed together about the great Messiah, but were overheard by a Roman, who also gave information about St. Canaan. He was then ordered to have a copper tongue full of poison fixed in his mouth; but his keeper, Donald M'Donald, had often heard him talk of the Messiah, and was almost persuaded to be a Christian; and having a respect for him, he often released him in the night, by taking this copper tongue out of his mouth. At this time the Lord endowed Saint Canaan with the spirit of prophecy, and he revealed to his keeper and fellow-sufferers that he was to die, but told them to rejoice at his death, as he was going to glory, but to bear in mind that they would never see Jeremy's Land, and the Lord would bring about their deliverance. The old saint then called for James M'Laren, his other keeper, and told him he would now leave the charge of his two helpless daughters upon him, and also the charge of the two daughters of the martyr who was last put to death, namely. Murdoch; and also that what the Lord had given him in secret should be made public. He then told James that the Lord had made known to him that it was the crown of Solomon he was in possession of, and that it should never be worn by the seed of a Roman, but that it should be worn by the seed of Abraham, and that Christianity was to flourish under it, in a renowned kingdom, above all other earthly kingdoms. James M'Laren was astonished at hearing these words of the saint, for he had kept the finding of the crown a profound secret. The saint also said—" When the storm shall arise be not afraid, for the Lord shall bring you deliverance." So Saint Canaan died, and immediately a storm rose so mightily that all those who did not believe in the prophecy departed, and fled to their boats for safety, whilst Saint Chaldea, who was chained to the dead saint, lifted up his voice and blessed the Lord, and said—"Stand steadfast in the faith, for the Lord will deliver us according as it was said by the saint." At this time the Roman sailors lost all hopes of safety, and fled to their boats, and were drowned whilst making attempts to get ashore. The only one of the Romans saved was Noustinous, the Roman slave merchant. He had gone down to his department for some treasure, and was left behind. He went to the helm of the vessel to steer it to Jeremy's Land; but James Mackay told him that the vessel went well when the Lord was at the helm, and they went on praising the Lord for their deliverance. So upon the third morning they landed within sight of Saint Laurence' Altar Hill, called the Hill of God, but now Dundee. The royal slaves took ashore with them the two daughters of Canaan, Mary and Helen; also Elizabeth and Dightus, the daughters of Saint Murdoch, who was martyred for Christianity by the way; also the body of Saint Canaan, which they buried near to Carnoustie. The daughters wept and mourned over their father three days, after which they fitted themselves with what was in the ship, and took their departure. Donald Mackay of the Law went back to the ship, and said—" As for thee, Noustinous, 'cur' thou there!" So the place is called Curnoustie to this day. It was thought that he had smitten him. James M'Laren upon the second day came to the hill where his father's altar stood, and where his father had offered sacrifice under the old faith, and said—" Would that I had a lamb to offer a sacrifice." But Saint Chaldea rebuked him, and said unto him—" Is thy faith so very weak after all the wonders which thou hast seen at Jerusalem, and thine own miraculous escape during our voyage, that thou wouldst insult the blessed Saviour, who came and offered himself a sacrifice for us all, and to make atonement for our sins, which no other could do. Thou canst pray unto God without any bloody sacrifice." So they all entered into prayer. That night they abode at the Altar Hill, as one of the daughters named Dightus had taken very ill. She died that night by the side of a river, which was then called after her. The other three virgins then took their way with the royal slaves and Saint Chaldea further west, nearer the mountains, seeing the country had all been laid waste by the Romans. James M'Laren essayed to go and see his mother's brother, M'Intyre of Kinclaven, and likewise Donald M'Donald, the crowned prince of Forteviot. They came near to their uncle's house, and found that all was laid waste and desolate by fire. Nothing could be seen about the whole premises but one old frail woman, who said unto them—" What do you seek? I have given you all that I had; I have nothing more to give you."

But Donald M'Donald, the Prince, said unto her—"We seek nothing from thee; we want to know what has become of our uncle." Then she said—"How can you call him uncle, seeing you are all Romans?" James M'Laren answered—"I am the son of Mary M'Intyre, his daughter;" and the Prince said—"I am the son of Jean, his eldest daughter." She answered—"If you speak truly, who are these with you?" They replied—"These are the two sons of M'Kay of the Law, and the son of Adam of Adamsdale, the grandson of king Donald of Port David. The rest of our young men were slain at Jerusalem. These three damsels are fellow-sufferers; and this is St. Chaldean, a preacher of the new times, and a servant of the blessed Messiah." She then said—"If your stories are all true (and I have no cause to doubt), you are too long here, lest the Romans come and see you, as they are ranging about for food." She then went a small way into a wood and made some signal, when there appeared two armed men in the costume of the Gaul; but seeing the men dressed as Romans, they started back and cried—"Have you sold us!" She waved her hand to them, and said—"They are your kinsmen; be not afraid." With that they took the royal party into a cave, and provided them with all things necessary. So upon the third day, there was a young man sent to the camp of Isaac, the son of King Donald of Port David, and brother to Donald the slave, to inform them that they had brought with them a saint who spoke many good things, and gave full report of the blessed Messiah having come on earth. St. Laurence of Laurence, and Comrie, and Neish, and the chief of the Grahams agreed that they should come forward; but the chief of the M'Intyres said—"No, they are spies; we had better put them to death, rather than allow them to return to the Romans, as they are come to see what our strength may be." But the chiefs and rulers said—"Let the men come forward; they may be telling a true tale." The women were desired to remain behind in the cave, but they would not, intimating that they would follow them even to death. So they prepared themselves, and marched to the Camp upon the top of Birnam, where the mountaineers were fortified. When they were brought forward they were placed before the whole of the rulers, and Isaac, and the priests of the congregation. M'Intyre then said they were spies, and insisted on them being put to death, but was opposed by the rest of the camp. St. Chaldean seeing M'Intyre, and knowing his heart, turned to him and said— " It is as true as that your wife will be brought to bed this night of an Ethiopian black and a leper, and for forty days thou shalt not see them;" and immediately he was struck blind. M'Intyre was by this still more enraged, and would have killed St. Chaldean with his own hand; but as he was blind he could not see him. The report came in the morning that the prophecy had been fulfilled, and there was born unto M'Intyre a child without one spot of white upon his body, and another, a leper, spotted like the calf of a deer. The chief was now even more enraged, and even called him a devil for fetching torments upon the people. So that all the camp believed it of him, and ever after had an aversion to him. Shortly before this, the clans had gained a complete victory over the Romans, upon the night which they held sacred to the memory of Romulus, the founder of pagan Rome. The clans had attacked them, and driven them to the other side of the river then called St. Laurence, but now called the River Tay. They fled to the wooden bridge they had erected, which giving way, many hundreds of the Romans met with a watery grave, and those who returned met with death from the clansmen's swords. The enraged Romans then collected soldiers from Ardoch, Adamsdale, and Callander, and all the other camps, to attack the clans. They were all in good spirits, at a place called Murthly. The clans then said— "They will be upon us by to-morrow." St. Chaldean, speaking in the Latin tongue, and interpreted by Donald of the Law, said—"Trust in the Lord, and he will fight your battle, for yonder camp of mirth shall be turned into mourning before to-morrow." He then told them to flee to the rocks which are called Raithallian, or the Chaldean race, " for the Lord," continued he, " will send amongst your enemies a plague, even from the time of the cock-crowing until dawn. Cover ye yourselves with your upper garments, and cry earnestly to the Lord, and he will deliver you." So they all fled at the command of the saint, and covered themselves with their upper garments or plaids. Early next morning the saint arose and ascended to the top of the Hill of Birnam, and looked toward the plain, which was covered over with a thick dark mist, so that he could not see nor hear one of the Romans, all was so still and quiet. But when the mists began to clear away, the desolated camp came in view. The horses were standing riderless outside the camp, with none to look after them. The clans then took possession of the camp, and the rest of the Romans fled beyond the River of St. David, now called the River Earn. A great terror fell upon all the clans after witnessing the dreadful judgment of God upon the Romans, so truly foretold by the prophet Chaldean. St. Chaldean then changed the Sabbath from the seventh to the first day of the week, and began to baptise in the name of the Father, Son, and Holy Ghost, so that the Lord might bless them and sanctify them by the Holy Ghost, through the washing of water. Isaac at this time arose from his seat, and placed his brother Donald the slave upon it, and crowned him king, this making him the first crowned king. Isaac chose rather to be servant to the saint than to be ruler or king; and forty-two days afterwards he was baptised and married to the daughter of Saint Canaan, and the place, situated to the back of Birnam, is called Kingsford to this day. The next baptised was James M'Laren, and he was married to another daughter of Saint Canaan. Then was married Donald M'Kay to the daughter of Murdoch, who suffered martyrdom on the passage from Rome to Jeremy's Land. Adam, son of Adamsdale, was baptised, likewise his wife, the sister of the rebellious M'Intyre, who was the founder of clan M'Adam, or Eadie in the Lowlands. James M'Kay and another sister of M'Intyre were also baptised, after which James M'Kay and this sister were married. They were the founders of the Gows of Athole, or Smith in the Lowlands. M'Intyre had his eyesight restored, and seeing his sons and the judgment of God, came to serious repentance, and was baptised, and became an eminent preacher of the Gospel of Christ. The religion of Chaldean spread so rapidly that in less than six months there was not one altar fire burning. They then took upon themselves the name of the Chaldeans, now called Caledonians, St. Chaldean being the founder of the Caledonians. They called the place Athelia, but it has now got the name of Dunkeld, after their holy saint. The first church known to be built for the doctrine of Christ was erected at Dunkeld. The north side of the River St. David, now called River Earn, was called Caledonia; and the south side being occupied by the Romans, was called the Italians' kingdom, and went also under the name of Fife. M'Laren then returned to his native town Dundee, with all his clan, and built a church for the doctrine of Christ there, and became a preacher. There were born unto him sons and daughters. The firstborn was called Laurence, after his father, and the second was called Canaan, after St. Canaan his father-in-law. For about thirty years the Romans had possession of the lands south of St. Laurence River, now called the Tay, the Palace of Forteviot, the lands of M'Kay of the Law, of Adamsdale, and the Forest, now called Auchterarder; and nothing grieved the clansmen more than seeing the lands of their forefathers in the possession of the Picts, Scots, Danes, and Romans.

When king Donald the slave died near Logierait, the nation was left to king Kenneth, the second son. The old slaves were now nearly all dead, and so were the old warriors who had sworn that they would not draw the sword whilst the Romans kept the truce and did not molest them beyond the Earn. The young king Kenneth being crowned king of Caledonia at Logierait, immediately sent for his cousin Kenneth M'Laren, son of James the slave, and told him that he would summon all the clans from the east to the west of Caledonia, and see if it was possible to clear the Romans beyond the Forth, and free their ancient country. Kenneth immediately accepted the offer. St M'Isaac, the king's uncle, proposed first to consult St. Chaldean, who then advised them to wait a season until God's will should be clearly revealed. The proposed war was therefore stopped for the time. At this time the Romans compelled their slaves to carry up earth and clay to the King's Altar Craig, now called Craigrossie, to make terrace gardens, such as they have in the Italian mountains. They occupied the king's hunting-tower, for the safe custody of their slaves from escaping. The camps lay in the valley of Adamsdale, with huts made of clay for their dwellings. All south of the Earn paid tribute to the Romans, being held in terror by the declaration that unless they brought sheep, or whatever was demanded of them, they were counted as disloyal, and put to death; even if asked they had to give up their fairest ones at the word of the tyrannical Roman Governors. Upon one evening, supposed to be Romulus' night they debauched themselves with wine which they had made, and during the night the mounds of earth which the slaves were forced to carry up, fell upon the Romans, and covered up the whole of the Roman army encamped there, none being saved from death except the slaves. Immediately after, king Kenneth passed over, and put Abernethy to the sword. The M'Kays thereupon crossed the King's Pass at Forteviot, and put all the Romans remaining at the palace to the sword. All the Romans north of the Forth fled in disaster beyond Bo'ness and Dumglass. King Kenneth was then crowned at Abernethy, with the crown that James, his father, had carried from the destruction of Jerusalem. He commenced immediately to build churches, the first he built being Cambuskenneth. The Romans then broke through the dyke, but were immediately attacked by the Grahams, assisted by the M'Kay's, Neishes, Comries, and the clan Cattan, a branch of the M'Kay's. They compelled them to march three days clear off their borders into the Scottish territory. Caledonia then flourished like the green bay tree, with religion, laws, and prophecy. Kenneth gave the second son of Comrie a place called Comrie Castle, in Fife, for his share of the booty; Neish received Borrowstounness, south of the Forth; the son of St. Laurence, of Laurence, received Laurenceston; Graham got Grahamston, near Falkirk; Arthur son of Arthur of Glenarton, got Arth south of Perth; Keir got Carswater, now called Carron. They spread their clans thus from east to west, and were growing fast into a mighty nation. King Kenneth of Fife now began to build a castle near Donree, now called Dollar. John Milne, son of King Donald of Forteviot, got a grant at Lochleven of a place called Milnathort-the-Muir; his brother Collin got a place to the west of this called Collin's Vale, or Coleross Abbey, of which he was the founder, and the first father of the ancient race of the Colegauls. For a long period everything went quiet, and every one could, without the use of weapons, visit their friends or acquaintances at a distance. Kenneth was married to the daughter of St. Lennox of Dumbarton. The first son was called James, after his father the slave, and the second son Kenneth, after his grandfather, the saint who died on the voyage. Donald Keir M'Donald, a kinsman of the king, was married to the daughter of prince Alpin of Duplin. At this time the country was again disturbed by a party of robbers, called Fenians, who were encouraged by the Romans to plunder the clans. The Caledonians were therefore again obliged to resume their warlike appearances. The M'Donalds were headed by their king, Kenneth M'Donald, who lived at Forteviot, in his father's ancient palace. Every clan again resumed their own banners, and resolved to avenge the murder of Keir and the plunder of Castle Comrie, and also the carrying away of a child from the same, as well as the murder of Graham of Grahamston and the Arthurs of Arth. The Grahams being so enraged at these acts of atrocity, broke through the Dyke at Kilsyth, and immediately put the Romans to the sword, and pursued them with much spirit. They were joined in the attack by the M'Lintocks, for the murder of their kinsman, who was a Waldense. These pursued them with so much vigour, that they repaid the Romans dearly for all the inroads which had been made upon them, and retook all the cattle and spoil which they had carried off. After driving them out of Caledonia, and plundering the half of Scotland, they returned with a heavy booty. Every clan went to their own parts, and St. Michael got the grant of Dumfries or Prince's Hill, and his descendents are considered to be the Carmichaels of East End House, being the east end of Caledonia. The Lennoxes once more occupied their native land, Lennerick town and castle. The Romans were so incensed by this defeat that they cursed their gods, and resolved that they would no more return to this place, unless they got Goths and Vandals who could withstand the cold. King Kenneth returned into Fife with peace and plenty. M'Kay of the Law, Clan Cattan of the Forest, and the Waldense of Gleneagles returned to their homes in peace. Every clan went to where the altars stood upon every Sabbath morning, to praise the Lord. The saint read the New Testament in Latin, he having an interpreter. Their creed was the Lord's Prayer; and their law was founded on the ten commandments, as taught by St. Chaldean. Every elder gave in his report of his own people to the saint and ruler. Every man that was baptised got land according to his needs; for they were not baptised until they gave satisfaction to the saint and elders of the Congregation. Any woman confined in childbed, when restored sufficiently, attended the preaching and prayers of the saint, which were especially intended for her good. She, along with the father, went to the saint and elders to deliver her child, that it might be fulfilled what the Lord said while on earth—"Suffer little children to come unto me, and forbid them not, for of such is the kingdom of heaven." It was then named by the saint, and when grown up was baptised according to his faith, and afterwards was married and received his land from the rulers, and was a joint member in the Church of Christ. If he re-married an outlaw pagan, he was immediately cut off from all his lands and connection with his clan, and never again was acknowledged by them before he first showed works fit for repentance, when he was again received into the Church. This was the custom of Caledonia for many years. King Kenneth was both a king and a preacher, and had prayed for the spirit of prophecy, but was denied. Saint M'Isaac, who chose to be a follower of Saint Chaldean, sent for the king, and told him that he had asked a foolish thing, seeking to be equal with the Messiah, and ordered him to stand a rebuke for his ambition before several of the saints, as no man could answer his prayer. The king departed wrathfully, but did as he was bid by the saint, and was again united to the Church, and became more zealous for the doctrine of Christ than ever, teaching, preaching, and baptising. He finished the building of Cambuskenneth, and preached the Gospel therein as an Established Church. His son, Kenneth the second of Fife, was successor to the kingdom, and was also a preacher of the Gospel like his father. The King came again to his cousin, King Kenneth of Forteviot, who was thought dying, and took charge of his son.

King Kenneth did not long survive his cousin. These are the stated facts, according to Saint M'Isaac, who wrote in the Latin.

The prophecy of Saint M'Isaac upon his deathbed at Callander. Calling his son, Saint M'Isaac the second, he said—" Son, take unto thee thy pen, and write this that the Lord hath shown unto me, for it lieth heavy at my heart that I neglected the words of Saint Chaldean, who died at Dunkeld. But the Lord hath brought it back to my memory by a vision, saying, Beware of the man-made priest, who shall come in as a wolf, not by the door, but shall come from afar upon thee, forcing himself upon thee by the claim of unrighteousness, and selling the Word of God for gain. Unjust decrees shall pass from his lips, and he shall pretend to cleanse others whilst he lieth in the mire himself. He shall speak fair words to kings, while he putteth the saints to shame, and even to persecution and death. But fear not when that cometh on the Church, as it is only a trial of your faith. Stand ye steadfast; for the Lord shall be your deliverer. By falsehood, guile, and fraud they will crown kings, and woe be to Caledonia when the seed of my sister cometh to the throne, for few shall be their days of reign, and bloody shall be their winding sheet. They shall drink of the abominations and idolatry of the scarlet woman ; they shall lie as wolves waiting and thirsting for the blood of the saints. But I say, fear not ; blessed is he who shall endure to the end, for the crown of glory shall be his. [This is believed to refer to Mary M'Donald, sister to the saint, who came back from the Romans with the steward of the camp, the first founder of the Steward family of Bute.] To prove this prophecy there shall arise a mighty champion of the Church, who shall appear even as a champion at arms, and shall be betrayed like our Saviour, for they will sell the godly man for gain. [Supposed to be Sir William Wallace.] The times shall be so troublous that a M'Donald shall weep over a M'Laren's grave, whilst there is none to comfort him. There shall be great tribulation in the land, for the scarlet-clad woman shall dress herself as a bride preparing herself for her bridegroom ; and with her smiles and guile she shall betray many, even so far that the one son shall betray the other, the father the son, and the mother the daughter. The forerunner of this prophecy shall be the falling of the king from his horse, and when there shall be none to fill his seat. [This is supposed to be Alexander the Third.] The chiefs shall turn so treacherous to their clans that they will even sell them to their enemies, and banish them from their own country. But the Lord will still be with you, although it will be only in the dark that ye dare worship Him ; even so much shall ye be persecuted and pursued from cave to cave, like as the eagle pursueth his prey. The Grahams shall turn traitors to the M·Donalds, and the M'Kays shall deny them; even treachery, robbery, and fraud, shall be their principles. There shall arise another king in another kingdom, who shall from his lust and abominations form a religion and call it godly. He shall deceive thousands until it shall be established, and shall sting Caledonia three different times ; but the Lord will yet deliver you. This prophecy shall be proved when a woman shall arise from the dead, and shall bear two sons of the true seed of King Kenneth of Fife, and they shall both be preachers of the Gospel. This proves that the cloud of God's wrath is passed over the Church for a time. [The prophecy was fulfilled at the births of Ralph and Ebenezer Erskine.] The chiefs will annihilate the country by being false unto their clans, and shall disperse them to a far foreign land, but the Lord shall be with them, and shall make them a nation, strong, and, like the Israelites, shall return them to their native land, and shall deliver the country from the deceiver. The ministers of the Gospel shall turn so slothful that they cannot carry the word of God from their breakfast table to the sanctuary. To prove this prophecy the streams of Glengyle shall wash the streets of the Grey Dogs Town, and shall turn over the causeway blocks with the current of the stream." The son then got wroth at the saint, saying—"Father, thou art beside thyself, seeing that Glengyle is at the west of Loch Katrine, and such a town as thou art speaking of, one never heard of ;" but the old saint in wrath rose to his elbow, and said—" There shall be such a town, and the Greyhound's Hunt shall be given to one of the true sons of Saint Laurence. This prophecy shall be fulfilled." The saint spoke no more to his son in prophecy. He died, and was buried at Callander, at the Clear River side.

King Kenneth was married to a daughter of Saint M'Isaac, the First, and was the father of twelve eminent preachers and a king. His firstborn was called Kenneth, who was the crowned prince; his second was Isaac; his third was Parlin, the founder of Dunfermline; the fourth was Saul, whose land was called Saline; the fifth was Cleish, or the swift man, who occupied the mountains, and was the first who burned coals; the sixth was Thomas, the founder of the Thomsons of Fife; the seventh was Saint Laurence, who went to Laurenceston, where his kinsman had been murdered; the eight was named James, and went to his kinsman Lennerick, where he was a preacher of the Gospel; the ninth was Chaldean, after the ancient saint who was the founder of the Chaldean Church at Kirkcaldy; the tenth was Donald, who was preacher of the Gospel to King Donald of Forteviot; the eleventh was M'Lour, the founder of the Clan M'Lour, who was a dwarf, and was a great horseman; the twelfth was named John. The Romans, being grieved at seeing the prosperity of the Caledonians, and not daring to attack them by arms, craftily brought some of their griffin eagles, which had been fed on nothing but human flesh, and thinking that they would destroy many of the Caledonians, sent them into the Oak Forests, now called the Ochils. Prince John, the youngest son of King Kenneth, journeying to Cambuskenneth, had provided himself with the hide of a bull, in which he clad himself, placing a knife called a skeen in the top of his tarbot or bonnet, and took another knife in his hand. He was attacked by one of these birds of prey. It having pounced upon him from on high, it received through its body the knife which was placed on his head, and with the one in his hand he soon despatched it, and severing the head from the body, carried it home in triumph to his father, who cried—"Bless the boy! what has he killed the bird with?" when he replied—"A skeen! a skeen! a skeen!" "'Askeen' from this day shall be your name," replied his father; "and ye shall either have as much land as may be measured by a hound's hunt or a hawk's flight." He having chosen the hawk's flight, it alighted on a stone, called, as interpreted, "My John's Stone," now called Clackmannan. He was the founder of that eminent family of

Alloa and Mar, named Askeen, or Erskine, this being the true son of Kenneth, and Ralph and Ebenezer being descended from him, fulfilled the prophecy of the saint with regard to them. Caledonia was at this time in a really flourishing condition. Cleish, the king's son, who was building a residence for himself, fell upon a black rock, and built part of his dwelling with it. Some of the black rock coming in contact with the fire, it ignited, and almost levelled his house with the ground. This accident led to the use of coal as fuel. The clansmen spread east and west throughout all Fife. Donald, King of Forteviot, went to King Kenneth the Second of Fife, and said—" Our fathers have agreed, and I likewise require no tribute from you, if you will please to grant me the breadth of one furlong of ground for a road between my two dominions, North and Western Caledonia, which grant he instantly received, and the place was called the King's Cairn Ferry, where there was a boat placed for the benefit of his two dominions, where all civilised subjects were allowed to pass and repass unquestioned, the boatman having a free keep for his wage from the king. This was to continue through all ages while wood grew and water flowed. Parlin, the son of Parlin of Dunfermline, was married to a daughter of Saint Lennox, and received with her a piece of land on the banks of Saint Lennox Lake, now Loch Lomond. They were the founders of the M'Farlanes of Arrucher, a fierce and warlike race who long kept these mountains. His son returned to his grandfather, and was taught all the rules of the Church, and became a preacher of the Gospel at Luss, after the death of Saint M'Isaac the second. When he went to the church to preach the word of God, he found the image of Saint M'Isaac, with a book before him, which in wrath he immediately seized and pitched into the lake, and rehearsed the first and second commandments unto them. [By making enquiry, the saint has been found, and is in Sir James Colquhoun's burying ground, with the book in his hand.] St. Parlin was preacher for many years in this place. The oldest college was at Dall, and was called St. Chaldean's College. The next was a college founded on the braes of the Divine, now called Aberuthven, for the benefit of the M'Kays and M'Donalds of the Royal Palace of the Isle, now called Gaskhall or Orchard, which was the royal residence many a day for the kings during any invasion. The M'Kays spread to the north and east, where they married and inter-married, and also preached and baptised in the name of the Lord. There was a son born to King Donald, whom he called Angus, who was sent with a large army to build Brechin Castle against the Danes, and watch the east coast against any invasion. There went with him Murdoch, who was married to Margaret M'Donald, daughter of King Donald of Forteviot, and was the founder of the M'Murrays in the Highlands, and Morrisons in the Lowlands, and cousins to the Gows of Athole, who were called Smith in the Lowlands, from their trade being of that description. One day while Gow was melting ironstone in a clay pot, his furnace was not strong enough, and it therefore burst, and he found the whole of his labour in vain, and in wrath left the place and all the other things to his servants. The son some time after, being travelling about, picked up a bit of the iron which had been melted, and which he got among the ashes. He tried to beat it, and at last succeeded in making it into the form of a hatchet. The king then got helmets and breastplates made of it, as nothing could pierce it, and they also made spears and other instruments of the same material. By this time every person was ordered to collect ironstone, and provide for the Gows of Athole swords and spears. In a very short time the whole nation was provided with it, which made their weapons more light and deadly. No foreign enemy durst attack them with their broadswords. Every clan throughout the whole of the north were very soon in possession of the same deadly weapons, and lived many years unmolested, till about the fourth century. The Romans then landed a mighty army in Fife, killing all the Blythes, the Melvilles, and the Macomishes, the plot being carried out by some of the Scots nation, who were well acquainted with the place. The clans were driven back with great loss, and King Kenneth was slain along with all his house, except one daughter who had been away at the Hunt in Dollar, now called Castle Campbell, which was built by Kenneth the Third for a royal hunting tower. She and her maids of honour seeing that the Caledonians were defeated, and had fled before Gastinius, with great loss of life, made the secret known to a forester whom she met with, that the crown of her father was concealed in a private vault in the Hunting Tower, having been laid there for fear of being discovered. This forester turned out to be one of the Erskines, who was faithful to her cause. She wanted to go to the west to meet with her father's clan at Balquhidder, but the Romans being all spread over the country, they went and got the crown, which Erskine, in the garb of a forester, carried, whilst she and the maids followed closely behind. When Donald of Forteviot heard the news, he immediately fled beyond the Tay, and she was faithfully conducted by Erskine, who was afterwards called "Donald, the Crown Protector." She was welcomed with great warmth by her kinsmen, and deeply lamented over the death of her father and so many of her gallant clan, none having escaped save the Deaf Prince. M'Lour escaped, although most of his clan were killed. Immediately all the clans were called back to Dunkeld, where the Royal Parliment was. The Romans had not ventured to cross the swamps of the Earn, but took possession of the whole of Fife, which they called their own Kingdom. Once more the fire towers were all put in order. Abernethy, Dunning, Turluam, and Muthall, were again all occupied by the Romans. Immediately the clans were called to their chiefs, and their cattle driven back into the Highlands, the clans being fully determined to give the Romans battle at the first opportunity. The report went to the King that his brother-in-law was slain, for the Romans were sparing neither man, woman, nor child. Lady Graham went to seek her murdered husband in the field, where she bare a son who was afterwards called St. Blare Graham, as he was born on the field of battle, and was the first founder of the family of the Blares. When the news reached the king, he arose from his seat in great haste, saying—"Every man now must do for himself, and God be with us!" He went to the top of the swamp which lay between him and the camp. Gastinius was engaged by dawn of morning by a furious onset of the clans, with the king and all their chiefs for their leaders. Gastinius had to fly, with dreadful slaughter, to his army, over the very field where he had triumphed as conqueror but yesterday, and was himself killed by the hand of Donald Graham's brother-in-law. They fled to Fife to regain their boats, and once more leave the Island, but a great number of them were captured by the Deaf Prince. They hung these prisoners at a place near the church of the Chaldeans. It was from the overthrow of Gastinius that Gask, in Perthshire, received its name, and a stone from the royal palace, called the "Boar's Stone," marks his head. There are some dates upon it in Egyptian characters, but not legible. This outbreak turned out badly for the Scots, as they saw that their trade was like to be endangered by the Caledonians, and that their peace was like to be disturbed. King Donald immediately gathered all his army to revenge the outbreak upon Fife, and the carrying away of their children and the murder of the noblest families, including the Deaf Prince, the brother of the murdered king Kenneth. The clans Waldense, Lennox, Arthur, and Niven, and James the Waldense, of Kennalther, who joined the M'Kays of the Forest, as his clan was but small, entered upon the Scottish Border, near Dumfries, with their saints and rulers at their head, and drove the Scots, Picts, and all the Romans who had intermixed with them beyond the river Between, now called the Tweed. For their own safety, the Romans immediately commenced to build a wall between Newcastle and Carlisle, and there was a space left between the two nations. Fergus the Seventh delivered himself up to Donald, saying—"It is better to be a cowherd to a decent man than to be a tormented king," for nothing but war and robbery was going on in his nation. Donald's heart immediately glowed towards the fugitive king, and he sent him and his wife and family back to the Lennoxes, for his safety from his own subjects as well as the Romans, who were hunting after him. Saint Johnston, of John's Town, now called Perth, said it was unlawful to leave a man unprotected who had thrown his life for protection upon them, lest he should be murdered and his blood demanded at their hand. Fergus was then removed to a place called Cool Fergie on the banks of St. David's River, now called the River Earn. He had the River Farg for fish, and Glen Farg for his forest.

The agreement between king Donald and the Romans was that if any of the latter passed over the Tweed they were liable to be hung, or otherwise dealt with according to the king's pleasure. This truce was made between the Romans, the king of England, and Donald, upon which, Donald withdrew his army from pursuit. The place called Thum-o'er-land lay between the two nations, neither having a claim upon it, except for the banishment of their outlaws. This divided the Scottish nation, one half belonging to England, the other half to Caledonia. Instead of the Scottish nation extending to the Tees water, it only extended to the Tweed, the English nation reaching Newcastle and Carlisle. Donald held his council at Dunfermline, but finding that all the books of the saint had been carried to Saint John's Town, he placed the Deaf Prince as prince and ruler of Fife, and of this man is the ancient race of M'Duff. He ruled so strictly that no Romans could be harboured in Fife. The King returned once more to Saint John's Town, covered with laurels, and seeing his kinswoman, the daughter of the late King Kenneth of Fife, he instantly proposed a marriage, and she was married to Donald, King of Caledonia, Fife, and Scotland—the first proclaimed King of the three countries. He was crowned with the crown of King Kenneth, which had been saved from the destruction of Castleton, near Dollar. The Erskines, the Queen's kinsmen, began to build a palace beyond the Tay, called Skeen Palace, and all prospered well with them for a considerable time. But the Romans could not rest satisfied after the defeats which they had received from Caledonia.

The Romans embraced Christianity at this time of a very different kind from that professed by the Caledonians. Collecting both Christians and pagans, which they called the "divers legions," they then provided them with all kinds of boats, and, in the summer season, occupied Norway, Iceland, and all places round the coast; and next summer landed upon the north coast of Scotland with such a mighty army that the Caledonians could not come against them, but were driven from their homes and native mountains, leaving all who could not withstand the fatigue of travelling to the mercy of these lawless robbers. By caution, all that belonged to the royal palace was hid in the rocks of Kinfauns, the Royal party leaving for their native residence at Logierait, beyond Dunkeld, on the banks of the River St. Laurence. But the Lord still remembered his ancient people, and put in the queen's heart a scheme for their deliverance; for many a fair and lovely woman had to submit to their abomination for the preservation of her family; and when a Dane left his staff at the door, the goodman durst not enter. She called all the saints' wives, and the wives of all the rulers in the nation, and told them she could deliver the country, and bring back their husbands to them, if they could only keep a secret. She told every one to provide herself with a knife, and those who had no knives were to be provided with one by the Gows of Athole, who were the royal smiths. They made what they called the queen's black knife, now well known in the Highlands as the skeen dhu. Every woman was provided with one, and sworn into the secret of the queen. On the night before Christmas, between twelve o'clock and the cock-crowing in the morning, every woman who had a Dane with her stabbed him under the fifth rib. The secret was kept and the deed was done, and the women of Caledonia claimed the highest seat in all public meetings. A certain part of each body had to be taken to the rulers' wives to certify that the men were dead, and that none were allowed to escape. On that night, the king, with the queen, was waiting for the crowing of the cock. The king made the remark that it must be a very cold morning, for the cock crew very hoarse. The queen replied—"Surely his throat need not be so dry, for he can wash it in Danish blood." The king not knowing the meaning of her words, asked their import, but was denied a reply. He then called his sentries and made enquiry, but they knew nothing. Coming back in a rage to the queen, he threatened her if she would not reveal the secret of her words, and drew his sword. She said—"Do what you please to a helpless woman, but to-morrow will reveal the secret if God has favoured our plan. The King neither slept nor went to bed, but watched on his towers, and about the dawn of morning, for which he had long waited, a man came running to the tower, exclaiming that there was not a Dane living in Athole, nor any other place that he knew of. This night was called the "night of the bloody blanket." The king went to the queen, and asked her pardon. She told him it was granted; but said if her uncle, the Deaf Prince of Fife, knew, he should not again present arms to her. He then asked for his breakfast, but she said—"Is it breakfast which you are minding? Mount sword and saddle, and set all your beacons on fire; collect all your scattered clans from the mountains, and spare not a man of the Danes who yet remain. This was called the "great secret" of the wise and beautiful queen Margaret. All his army being called, it was found that a good number of the Danes had escaped the snare so cleverly laid for them by the women. The Caledonians again formed themselves into an army, and every clan having gathered unto their different banners, a council of war was held at Dunkeld. It was resolved to attack the Danes before succour should arrive, and if possible to completely destroy them. Having travelled for three successive days, they at last met with some Danes, who were scattering before them in every direction. The Deaf Prince cleared all Fife, and having mustered about seven thousand men, joined the king's banner at Scone, the M'Kays of the Forest, or Auchterarder, swearing to the king that they would wash the cat's nose in the North Sea, after having dipped it seven times in Danish blood. The Danes seeing they were completely overpowered, cried to Mars, the god of war, but were closely pursued by the Erskines. They also tried to raise the spirit of Crue Mar, which was another of their gods, in their behalf. The queen was in person at the battle, with her kinsman, John Erskine, the Crown Protector of Caledonia; and he was created Baron of Mars. He was the founder of Skeen House, Aberdeenshire, the first house built with lime in that district. The king was then advised to suspend operations until summer, and returned to Perth. No more tribute nor respect was paid the Danes. They had even to steal some cattle for their support. The M'Murray's were so enraged at the treatment which they received from the Danes that they could not refrain from shooting the first Dane who came in contact with them. The Danes built a fort called Donnoter Castle, which was the only place of refuge they had beyond the river Ness. The clan Cattan abode with the Morrisons of Moray-shire, as they had sworn that they would not return until they had accomplished the complete overthrow of the Danes. Early next summer, the king called all his nobles to meet at Scone Palace, to support the clans Cattan and Erskine, who were standing as guards of the North. Every fifth man was chosen, and ordered to be under arms upon the fifth day of May; and whilst advancing they found that the Clan Alpine, now called M'Gregor, with the Erskines, the Morrisons, and the Clan Cattan, had put Donnoter to the sword. Very few escaped in their boats beyond the River Ness. The whole royal host then marched to the north, with twelve saints at their head, to free the northern parts from the Danish army. They were strongly opposed at a place called Isaac's Ferry. Saint M'Isaac fell that day upon the field; but next day they forced the pass, and reached a place called Mullbowie, where the Danes had encamped. The second day's fighting commenced immediately, with dreadful slaughter on both sides. The chief of the M'Donalds of Badenoch fell at the battle. The elder son and the king came lamenting, and said—" We have gained the island." The king said—" I have lost my best warrior; it is a black island to me." Full of revenge and grief, the second son cried out—" This is not a time to lament him; it is a time to avenge him. The loss of one M'Donald is not the loss of a battle. Let *rousett* be to us!" and then vehemently struck into the battle. His saying is interpreted, "Let the loss be to us." He was called M'Donald, Earl of Ross, and was the first Earl of Ross-shire. His son Robert got a place called Dunrobin. They pressed upon the Danes, and received great loss, because the Danes were supported by the Normans. They fought the battle of Killin, now Dingwall, and lost the chief of the Blythes, Saint Fillan, but still pressed on in the fight, the Danes losing ground, although the Norwegians were constantly strengthening them by supplies of men. They fought another battle called Killearn, with great loss upon both sides, the chief of the M'Larens of Dundee being slain. They advanced close to a lake called Lake Broom, and not being aware of the Danes being so close upon them, were immediately overpowered by numbers, and were driven back with great slaughter, and the king narrowly escaped. This battle was like to be gained by the Danes, as they had driven the clans back, but yet they never wavered nor left the field, and night closed the fight. During the night the king found that he had lost the chiefs of the M'Kays of the Law, and the Davidsons of Strathearn, and did not know what to do, as the clans were getting weaker, whilst the Danes were recovering strength. The Deaf Prince said to the king—" Allow the pipers to fall back with me, and be ready when we arrive at the camp to raise three cheers with a loud voice." So he went out, and came in, each time with the gathering tune of a different clan, the clans saluting him as already stated. The Danes believing from these signs that the whole clans were gathering in upon them, bethought themselves that their only safety lay in procuring their boats to make their escape out of the country. Many of them who had no boats were slain, and others fled to the mountains, and were pursued by the enraged clans. A small battle was fought, and Elgin was slain, at a place now called Glenelg. Elgin was the founder of the Elgins of Murray, and called the river after his wife, Lussey. The M'Kay then fulfilled his word, and washed the cat's nose in the North Sea, after having dipped it seven times in Danish blood.

The Danes were left in possession of the islands, whilst the clans possessed the mainland. The King made M'Kay lord and king of that country, to be free from all tribute, and to be as a bulwark to keep the country from the Danes and all her enemies. It was called Caithness, or M'Kay's Country. The King began to return back, and gave grants to those who had distinguished themselves, according to their valour. The Earl of Ross got the whole of that shire; his son was made Baron of Dunrobin; the second son of Neish got Inverness and the forest extending to Loch Ness. A bare, swarthy, skinny man, the son of Glass, the grandson of M'Laren of Inverlaurence, and grandson to Saint Lennox of Dumbarton, from his sharp keen looks, well-known by the name of Chissinglass, was married to the daughter of Baron Neish of Turluam, now called Drummond Castle. He was the founder of the Chissem family, his Christian name being unknown. The

M'Intyres got what was called M'Intyre's Fort, but now called Campbelltown. The king wished the Deaf Prince's son to take land in the north; but his father said, no, because the race of the M'Larens had got more land than they could occupy. Upon that, the king made M'Morrich Baron of Morayshire, to join with the M'Donalds of Spey Water. There was born unto him a son called Peter, who got from Petershead to join the lands of Erskine. This was the founder of the Patersons of Clanpatrick. The king arriving at Skeen House, Aberdeenshire, was informed that his beautiful and wise queen was labouring under bad health since the death of his eldest daughter. He arrived only in time to clasp her in his embrace before she departed this life. Her health had suffered from her exertions to raise an army to pursue the Danes. She left him, with one son and one daughter, to mourn her loss. She was the first laid into the sepulchre of Skeen House. There was a Chaldean church built near the Palace. The king mourned very much for his queen, and her uncle was likewise very much grieved at the loss. But the rulers and saints considered that the king would be better to choose another queen, as he was daily falling off with grief. He chose the daughter of Fergus, ex-king of Scotland. The saints opposed him, saying that it was not lawful to marry her, as she was not baptised, and did not believe in the Chaldean faith. Saint John, of St. John's Town, examined her and her father upon the Chaldean faith, and found them quite ignorant with regard to it. The marriage was postponed until she, with all of her father's house, could give satisfaction to the saints of the Chaldean Church, her father coming to learn the rules of the Church, with his daughter and all his family, stating that he was tired of Rome and all its principles. She was then baptised, and married to King Donald; but if his first wife was wise, this one was as foolish. Her first son was born, and called David, which was a leading name in Caledonia. She began to abuse Donald the crowned prince, and his sister being older was grieved at the usage to which her brother was subjected, but durst not speak for fear of subjecting herself to confinement. The Queen so ill-used the young prince that he was called "Daft Donald." The

boy grew up, and being looked down upon by every one at the
palace, grew very dull and slothful. His sister grew up, and was
married to the Deaf Prince, M'Duff. The young prince, when he
grew up, was sent to herd cattle, and durst not enter the palace
but as a servant. Time wore on until he became a pretty old man,
his father being now far advanced in years.

The Normans, after the death of the Deaf Prince, made a full
attempt with arms to take possession of Fife. They commenced,
for fear of defeat, to build a large city called after the Roman Saint
Andrew, quite contrary to the laws of Caledonia. They were so
well provided with both arms and soldiers from the Continent,
that the city was going on fast. M'Duff and his lady had again to
take shelter in Scone, having been driven out of Fife; and immediately the King's ambassadors were sent to rouse the different
clans. The prince, Daft Donald, asked his father if he might be
allowed to see a battle. "You fool," returned his father, "are
you tired of your life? Some people see more of them than they
wish." But as he still pressed upon his father, and said—" I will
remain by myself, and will go near none of you, so that you will
have no cause to be ashamed because of me," the queen said—
"Let the fool go; we can very soon get as good as he to drive in
and out the cattle." He was allowed to go, and told that his sight
would be short, meaning that very soon he would be killed. He
went into the armoury, and was insulted by the lowest of the
servants as well as the queen, they giving him some broken swords.
He went and struck their flat sides on the water until he got one
that would not break, along with a neighbour for it. He then
got a bull-hide dress made, and clad it all in the inside with sponge
of trees so craftily that if he was struck the sword would stick in
the sponge. He then repaired to his father's army, and was so disguised, keeping himself free from all, that few knew who he was.
The Normans were attacked at Bargona, a place for gathering
tythes for the city of St. Andrews. The battle began heavily, and
the ferocious Donald commenced at one end of the Norman ranks,
levelling rank after rank of the enemy, cutting round the king, and
showing his mighty strength of arm; and every one who struck at

him was sure of death, as the blades of their swords stuck in the sponge. So vigorously did he fight until the sun set, that the Normans were obliged to quit the field with great slaughter. After the battle was over, the heroic Donald pursued after the enemy, and several skirmishes ensued, until he singled out Rhone, their chief leader, and clave him with his sword from the right shoulder to the left haunch. The darkness of night set in, and found the Normans all scattered without a leader. The place is called Killing Rhone to this day, and is near to the Italian Slave Market, now called Cupar-Fife. Rhone's armour was silver, and many more of his chiefs were clad in the same costume. Next day, the king followed up the rear of his army, and a council of war was held at Melville Hill, and the king ordered them to return and to look after the wounded, and bury the slain. Looking round and seeing the warrior who had so greatly distinguished himself walking alone some distance from the camp, he sent a messenger for him; but he said, no, that it would break his oath to speak either to the king or to his sons. The king in wrath said—"What! such an answer! he has fought well, and wherefore should I not reward him? He replied—"I will answer when I am again herding the cows of the palace." The king looking towards M'Duff, the chief ruler of Fife, said—"Wot ye it is my eldest son Donald?" M'Duff being the brother-in-law of Donald, mounted his charger and rode up to him, and said—"Take off your bonnet, sir, if you please." He replied—"My bonnet contains three horse shoes." "What do you mean?" asked M'Duff. Donald then affectionately asked how his sister was, or if she was safe from the murderous Normans. The two noble warriors burst into tears, and embraced each other. M'Duff, taking hold of his sword, was about to swear by the God of Heaven that Donald should be crowned; but Donald forbade him, saying—"Swear not, for I am not saint-taught, neither have I been baptised. How then could I take the responsibilities of a crown upon me?" Donald was then taken back to his father the king, who said—"Donald Douglas, thou shalt receive whatsoever thou requirest." He said—"Give me for wife, when I am baptised, Helen, who washes the milk dishes in Skeen House;"

and drawing out his sword, he said—" Give me the lands of her father, M'Laren, who was murdered by the Danes. His wish was granted, and he went for twelve months to attend St. John of St. John's Town, and was baptised unto the Chaldean faith, she having been a member of the Church before. They took possession of Castle Awe, above Abernethy, and dwelt there. He was the founder of the Douglas family, and became Baron of Abernethy, and his descendents hold the title rights of Abernethy to this day.

King Donald from the fatigue of war died at Scone. He left instructions to bury him beside his beautiful queen Margaret, and not to bury his second wife near his remains. Douglas at this time was quite satisfied with the grant given him; so David, the grandson of Fergus, the second wife's first-born, was crowned king. He was very slothful, and cared little for national affairs, raising great companies of his nobles to play at ball and such like nonsense, which grieved the heart of Saint Johnstone very much; and he brought a decree out that all was fair and right at the ball of Scone, and though a man should have his life endangered, or even if he should be killed, the cause was never to be asked. The king became a real drunkard, and Saint Johnstone applied to get him dethroned, but through his vice and ill habits he died. Angus his brother was to be put in his stead, but the saints applied to the voice of the nation, and they chose a young man, the son of the heroic Douglas, as Douglas himself had refused the crown, not being saint-taught. This young man was the son of Helen, the Milkmaid, and Donald the Cowherd. All the nobles were ordered to meet at their ancient place of meeting, mounted with sword and saddle. There were a great many found like unto the slothful king; and a decree was passed that every chief was to call every month all his clan to a certain spot, and the chiefs had to appear twice before the King, with saint and servant, at a place behind the royal palace of Forteviot, called the Tilting Hill. The king's brother, James Douglas, could have hit a lady's ring forty feet above his head, whilst his horse was going at full speed.

A dispute arose in the palace because of the absence of King Kenneth's crown. The Deaf Prince being dead, they applied to

Erskine, the late queen's kinsman, who had been created guardian of the crown. He at once remembered having hid the crown, along with the royal ring and sceptre. St. Johnstone, who also knew its hiding place, being now dead, the whole of the secret with regard to the crown lay upon him. The king, with old Erskine, went to look for the place where it had been buried, but could not find it. Erskine requested them to take him in the dark; and they having done so under cloud of night, he came near to the spot by laying hold of the cliffs where he had gone before; and stepping upon a piece of ground in the cleft of a rock, he took the king's tilting spear, and placing it in the ground, he told them to search round that to-morrow, and then retired for the night. They came next day with the royal party, and by digging found the crown very near the spot marked out. The crown being taken up and cleansed, the cloth in which it was wrapped was found to be rotten, and was removed; but when taking the crown home, it was found that one of the diamonds had gone missing, and the royal ring, which the queen had attached to it with a cord, was likewise missing. They searched for the lost articles, but no account of them was ever found. The name which the place received was Ringhead, now Kinfauns. Douglas was then crowned with this crown, which they joined with a crown which had been sent by Titus to Jeremy, his kinsman, and was carried home by the royal slaves.

There was nothing happening at this time to disturb the peace of the country, except the Danes breaking in and stealing the sons of some of the leading familes, in order to have them taught in their own principles; but shortly afterwards the Normans that were in St. Andrews refused to pay any homage to the king, or to M'Duff, the ruling prince of Fife. They had got provisions and supplies from Normandy, and they broke out and put Fife again to the sword. The Caledonians again gathered every man to his own banner, and James Douglas, the grandson of Douglas of Castle Awe, seeing such an enormous army, did not attack them, thinking with the king that it was more wise to retire. There were great numbers of Romans amongst the enemy. They captured the son of Comrie, of Castle Comrie, and several others. By the king's command, the Caledonians fled beyond the Tay, and carried all their cattle with them, and burned all their other property which was left. Saint Fillans, the fourth chief of the Blythes of Fife, said—"The Lord will fight our battles; put ye your trust in Him." Saint Melville, the first of the Melville race who was a preacher, and Saint Collins, his kinsman, left nothing in Fife that could be carried off, but a few children and women. These the Normans sent to the Welsh market, as it was the only slave market in Britain at this time. The clansmen were all back in their mountains with plenty of cattle, fish, and deer, teaching and preaching the word of God according to the Chaldean faith, while the Normans, Danes, and Romans were daily dying from starvation. They at last returned to St. Andrews, which was their holy city, and remained there till next spring, when they intended to lay waste the mountains, and pursue the Caledonians to the utmost boundaries of the land. But the Lord was pleased to bring a mighty wind, and the sea rose so high that they could not get beyond the city; and during the night an earthquake was felt so great that Saint Fillans felt it west from Comrie, and going out and calling his clan, said—"The Lord hath done it. Go ye back to your country." They knew not what the saint meant; but a slave escaped from the Castle, and fled to King Donald at Scone with the report of the destruction of the city, and immediately James Douglas, the king's brother, mounted his horse, and raising his banner, rode for St. Andrews as fast as possible, to save the lives of the slaves. At twelve o'clock at night, the waves rose so high that they struck the walls midway, and the city instantly disappeared. The clan returned to Fife; but Saint Fillans said to his eldest son—"Thou art taught to be of the army of God and a servant of Jesus; give now the lands of M'Laren's Rock to thy second brother James, and tarry thou here among thy kindred." The ground which was occupied by the Saint still bears his name, Saint Fillans, near Prince David's Lake, now Loch Earn. There was great peace in the land for a long time, every mouth praising God for their deliverance. All Fife was again inhabited by its ancient inhabitants, who lived peaceably, a God-fearing and God-serving people.

At this time the prophecy of Saint M'Isaac was beginning to be fulfilled, where he speaks of the "man-made religion," contrary to the will of God, neither believing in baptising nor in the Lord's Supper, according to the rules of the New Testament, but placing mortal man the head and ruler, whereas they should have acknowledged the supremacy of God. The Romans saw that they were to be totally overwhelmed by Christians, and therefore made a form of Christianity to suit themselves. This had been about 666 years after the birth of our blessed Messiah. The founder of this doctrine claimed powers which belong only to God, and his priests pretended to cleanse and save people's souls, as foretold by Saint M'Isaac, while they themselves were lying in the mire; also that he should "trouble the Church with great persecutions, but blessed is he who endureth to the end. As the leaves fall from the trees of the forest, so shall he fall off, for his reign shall be one thousand two hundred years, when he shall lose his earthly power. And the kings of the earth shall be defiled by him, and shall pass many unjust decrees against the saints of God." With this object, a mighty army invaded a part of France, whose people had early received the word of God from the Waldenses. The Christians were sorely persecuted, but would rather suffer death than submit to their unrighteous demands. Many of the Waldenses fled to their kinsmen in Caledonia. Saint Monance fled into Fife, and built a church called Newarp, which is to be seen to this day. He was believed to be the first who introduced a complete copy of the New Testament. The English, Welsh, Irish, and part of the Scots, becoming jealous of the Caledonians, immediately ordered all that professed the Chaldean faith to depart from their territories under the penalty of instant death. They therefore fled before their persecutors to Caledonia. King Donald fearing an attack, gave them shelter, and sent them to the north to a place called the Lowlanders' Land or Dale, where they were granted land under the jurisdiction of the Earl of Ross and the Robertsons of Dunrobin. They became a brave and worthy people, true to the cause of their religion. The saints preached everywhere against the desolation and abominations which were like to come upon them. Holland being mostly peopled by Christian slaves from Jerusalem, suffered much from these persecutions, but still continued in the faith. Donald fortified all the Borders with the ancient clans, as he could not trust the Scots. He sent inspectors through the Borders, and found that there was very little doing in agriculture, ravage and murder being their principal employment, so that the place was very thinly inhabited. Berwick, the capital of Scotland, was nothing but a den of thieves, and the king and his brother, James Douglas, valiant and heroic as they were, got clear of them with great difficulty, The king then held his council at Edinburgh. One of the Scotts, who were the chief rulers on the Borders, drew a dagger, and made a thrust at the king's heart, in the Council room, whilst another tried to stab the heroic Douglas; but they had been clad in the armour of the Gows of Athole, which no sword or spear could pierce. They immediately got to their steeds, but an assassin made another attempt near to the gate. Douglas and the king did nothing until they were without the gates, where they followed him, and taking hold of the reins, demanded to see by whose authority he had presumed to come and question them, as they were the descendants of Queen Scotta, who had no right to answer such questions, and although their cowardly king left them, they were determined to fight for their country; and they threatened to hang Douglas and the king upon Calton Hill, upon the gallows tree, until their heels should kick the bark from it, and that their bones should be bleached as white as their shirts, if their necks should bear their bodies so long. Seeing that nothing remained but to defend themselves, they drew their swords, and soon cleared a way for themselves, their weapons being of the best steel, against which no mail could avail more than if they had been clad with leaves of trees. They then proceeded to Lennerick Castle, in Western Caledonia, where they were heartily welcomed by the Lennox clan. When the news was told to Saint Lennerick, he took a hearty laugh, and said—" How does your Majesty think that we can be tormented daily, when you cannot stay one night with them ?" The king then proceeded to Prince's Hill, now Dumfries, where his kinsmen told him that they could not keep a cow but it was in danger of being stolen. After returning to his palace at Scone, the king ordered every chief's second son to appear in armour, and if there were five in a family he took two. Raising all the clans, and marching to the south, Edinburgh was summoned to surrender, and the town was immediately given up. The king having asked what was the cause of the outbreak, they told him that the Scotts were a rebel party, who would neither cultivate the land themselves nor give others peace to do so. The king said he would allow none to hold lands but baptised members of the Church, as in Caledonia, and those who held them should be forced to cultivate them. He gave them forty days to qualify themselves, and at the end of that time those who had not conformed to the new laws had their lands confiscated by the king. There was little religion on the Borders, except Druidism, and a sort of paganism. They put their captives to torture with every kind of abuse, and afterwards put them in a cage and burned them, believing that the application of the remains was certain salvation to any one's soul. They practised this throughout Wales and all England for a long period. The sacrifice for a king or any great noble was generally put into a golden cage, and when the sacrifice was over, the Druid priest stained himself with the ashes of the human being burnt. For three nights he lay in this condition on the altar, taking possession afterwards of the melted cage. In this way they became possessed of nearly all the gold in the Welsh and English nations. There was a king of Wales called Arthur, who expelled them out of all his country, as the Church of Rome was beginning to spread her wings over these two devoted nations. The Druids then came down to a piece of vacant land between Scotland and England, and practised their rites along the Scottish Borders. Seven priests came bearing a human victim in a cage to King Donald. The King asked what the criminal had done to be placed in such a condition. Saint Lennox said—"They will sacrifice him as an atonement for your sins." The king ordered them to be brought up to him, and made the interpreter ask how long they had followed these bloody rites. They answered since the days of holy Scotta, Anglia, and Hibernia, and added that their fathers had made these gracious queens holy and good in heaven. The king said there was no time to parley with such stuff, and ordered the seven priests to be hung. He also ordered the cage to be broken open and the prisoner set free, and he gave him a blue ribbon to be a token that he was the king's beggar. This was the first of the "King's Beggars" of Edinburgh. The Druids then fled from King Donald, so that the Border was nearly vacated. There was not a Druid priest who did not fly. Having gone to Northumberland, they formed themselves into a nation, taking the name of Gypsies, with a king and queen over them. They became fortune-tellers, and were therefore called the "false," but afterwards the fause, or Faas. Many miles of the Border of the Tweed were left without a single inhabitant, so the king gave land to all his loyal subjects. The king's eldest sister, named Helen, was married to M'Donald, one of her own kinsmen, who got Helensdale; Elizabeth was married to one of the M'Larens of Gowrie; and Anne was married to one of the Saint Johnstons of Perth. Alexander M'Donald, the son of the Prince of Forteviot, got a place called Armsdale. He was distinguished from the rest by his enormous strength of arm, and was therefore called Armstrong. The Border was peopled by all the clans. David, a kinsman of the king, got Teviotdale. The king placed saints to preach the Gospel along the Border. He then returned to Scone.

The Pope, having made several unsuccessful attempts to induce the Caledonians to submit themselves to him in spiritual matters, at last gathered a mighty army with about two hundred priests at their head, under one holy Saint Divine, with a sword of blessing and a coat of valour, and a large feather dipped in blood, so that he was never to be conquered. St. Divine swore by the holy Pope that he would bring the last Chaldean in chains. He sailed to Britain, and landed at a place called Port Divine, now Devonport. He presented the king of Britain with a sword of victory, a coat of bliss, a red feather dipped in blood, and a large red griffin to go in the front of his army. Summoning Ireland, Wales, and England to turn out to his banners, the army was so large that they were scarcely able to get food. This news reaching Scotland, Donald as quickly as possible was on the Border himself. By his orders, all the cattle and deer were driven beyond the Forth, and all goods removed, leaving not so much as a single hut to shelter the enemy. When they arrived, the Gypsies were all plundered, but this only served them during one night. There was a great store sent into the Clyde, but the Lennoxes, Arthurs, M'Farlanes, and M'Gregors, with the Stewarts of Bute, and the M'Nairns of Arron, were on the alert, and when the sailors came ashore to look for the Roman camps, the clans, under the command of Saint Lennox of Dumbarton, put them to the sword, and taking their boats, immediately boarded their ships, and slew all who were there. All the clans of Fife, with horses carrying bags, repaired to the Clyde as fast as possible, and very soon emptied all the vessels into northern Caledonia. Five men were discovered apparently looking for the ships. They said they were Gypsies; but Saint Lennox said—"Get them a horn, they will make us spoons;" but they could not, so they were hanged on a green oak tree, to prevent them carrying tidings to the enemy. The place is called Greenoak even to this day. It was a great disappointment to the Romans to find some of their ships sunk, and the rest driving about at the mercy of the waves, all empty, and none to give the account of what had happened. After the long march, the holy Divine with all his army were left doubting the Divinity of the Pope, in not foreseeing all this sad disaster; while the Caledonians were left alone in their fastnesses praising God, and looking strictly for spies and vagrants. The winter closed upon the Romans at a place called Claudius' Huts, now Glasgow. So grievous was the winter that the one, looking in the other's face, saw nothing before them but death from cold and hunger. They got some of the old ships and sailed to Ireland, and some of the Western Islands were completely laid waste by them. The people of Arran and Bute fled to the mainland, and joined the clans.

The Romans completely destroyed Columba's Church in Iona. That holy saint's history is entirely lost. He was a follower of Christ, and likewise a great prophet. He was persecuted from island to island, and was believed to be one of Paul's followers. This celebrated saint was so sorely persecuted that he prayed to the Lord to send him to some barren island, where he might raise a church to His glory. He was sent to Iona. Visiting the mainland, he fell in with some followers of Saint Chaldean, who could discourse with him, as they held the same principles. He said he would like to see the place of Saint Chaldean, meaning Dunkeld. They found nothing in their travels but Christians believing in the rules of the New Testament. The Saint and his guide asked a woman by the road side, near Dunkeld, where was Saint Chaldean's Church. She had a child who was crying, having been scalded by the heat. The child was miraculously healed by St. Columba. He preached the Gospel of Christ for thirty-one years, and died at a place called Kilmacomb. The whole of Saint Columba's Island was afterwards turned into a Roman Monastery by the Irish and Romans. Many of the Roman faith have been there, and taken upon themselves the name of the island.

Early in the spring they all returned back to their camp once more, and joined their march towards the north, with fresh provisions and supplies from Rome. The Chaldeans were all in warlike order, and opposed the advance of the Romans at a place called Glendevon in the Ochils. The Caledonians made a furious onset, with their steel weapons, while the enemy having only copper, the battle went sore against them. They had to alter their line of march, and fell back towards the plains. The Lord brought his hand against the progress of the Romans by sending thousands of mice upon their stores. Saint Divine, or Devon, having been slain, and the chiefs seeing that it was impossible to advance any further against such deadly weapons, they returned to the plains, where they held a council of war, and resolved that they would withdraw from that mountain. The Caledonians called a council, and thought it advisable to fall back beyond the swamps of the Earn, with all their cattle and goods, so that they would be more fit to cope with their strong foes. The next morning, the Romans, seeing the clans had left, cried—"The foe's away!" The place is now called Fossaway. The Romans, thinking that the Caledonians had fairly given up the pursuit, and fled to their separate grounds, again put themselves into array, and took the mountain pass, but the Caledonians had been across all the field carrying away all their dead and burying them, so that the Romans could not ascertain their loss. They also carefully gathered their broadswords and daggers, which were made of steel, for fear of them falling into the hands of the enemy. Then all the saints fell upon their knees, and prayed that the Lord might be pleased to turn their foes away from them. The king stopped all the passes across the swamps, and was prepared for any emergency. Saint Fillans the Fifth came to him and said—"Shed no more blood, for the Lord will fight your battles, as he has done your fathers'." A great number of small animals, much resembling mice, came to all the camps of the Romans. Their bites were very venomous. Neither they nor the Romans crossed the River Earn, and these animals by their venomous bites soon overcame that mighty host. The Romans sent to the Pope an account of all their disasters, praying that he would intercede for them, and send his holy birds of Paradise with his blessing to them. The Pope was visited at home by a severe famine, so he sent word not to come back, except a few of the chiefs, leaving the rest to fight for themselves. He sent an ambassador to the Caledonians, saying that if they would call their country Scotland, he would never raise arms against them. Donald, answering the ambassador, said—"We care not what you call it, but we will preach the Chaldean faith, with the Lord's prayer for our creed, and the ten commandments for our law, and the New Testament shall be our guide and protector ; and if we find any of your priests preaching any other doctrine, as long as trees will grow we will not spare their necks.

The Roman army then broke up, but most of them remained in the country. They were called the Finguals or Fenians, and kept the country in a constant state of warfare. They took possession of a great piece of the west Highlands, as far north as Skye, calling it their own, and crowning kings, and appointing rulers at their own pleasure. They even came into the king's forests and the centre of the country, and carried off the cattle. Amidst these troubles the gallant King Donald died.

A young king then rose who was every whit as valiant as his father, and was called the fortunate King David. Calling his brother Donald, his father's second son, he said—" Raise every clan, and clear the country of these lawless rebels. His orders were immediately obeyed. Donald having gathered a few from every clan, took his march to the west and north-west. They had plundered Rannoch Forest, and defeated the clan M'Condochie, or Duncan in the Lowlands, and the clan Robertson, descendents of the royal family of the M'Donalds of Forteviot. O'Docherty plundered the forest of Lord Neish, and took possession of the Glen, which he called Glendochart after himself. They were so numerous that they almost overthrew the royal party. Donald and his army advanced within sight of the enemy; but, seeing that they were five times his number, he retreated upon the M,Gregors of Glenlyon, and the war was allowed to drop till after winter. All winter the clans were preparing cross-bows, as the Finguals fought with long clubs. They also got long spears with hatchets on them, called Lochaber axes, as their swords had no chance with the Finguals' long clubs. Next spring they marched upon the enemy, and a great battle ensued, the people being slain in great heaps on both sides. The battle was almost lost to the clans, when Lord Rae came to their aid with a party of the M'Kays, and swept the field. The Fenians seeing that the day was lost, threw their long cabers into a loch called Lochaber, or the Caber Lake, and fled, when a cruel slaughter was made upon them by the clans, the mountain streamlets running with blood everywhere. The M'Kays had boats which they brought from Caithness, and pursued the enemy, who fled to Normandy for safety. The young brother of the M'Kays, named John, being more daring and active than the chiefs, said— " I am out first," and claimed the land; but the Earl of Ross, one of the M'Donalds, seeing the young man's gallantry, said—" I will give you land; dispute not with your brother." They cleared the island of the Normans, and then asked for a strong clan to be placed there. The Erskines were nominated, as the M'Kays had enough to do to keep their own against the Normans. It was called Erskine's Isle, or the island of knives. Erskine got this for his part in the war, but it was still to be under tribute to the palace at Scone. John M'Intosh received a hound's hunt on the plains of the Black Island, and was married to Margaret M'Donald, the daughter of the Earl of Ross, and was the founder of the M'Intosh race. The prophecy which runs thus—

> "Truth and honesty from Caledonia will fly
> When M'Intosh in arms will meet the M'Kay,"

was fulfilled about the year 1315, at the battle on the North Inch of Perth, between the M'Intoshes and M'Kays. The M'Donalds got Morven, the seat of the Fenian king; the Rivens got a piece of land near Fort William; the Stewarts of Bute got Appin of Stewart; Alexander got Glengarry, and John got Glencoe, all being of the race of the M'Donalds; the M'Intyres got Loch Awe side; the M'Larens got St. Oban; the Raiths got Inverraith, now Inverary. The land was divided thus, for rewards of war, and every man was content with his allotment, and continued thus for some time. The Fenians were driven beyond the Clyde, which they called their father's share.

The Abbot of Northumberland Abbey, fled with the daughter of Lord Neish, and gained her liberty, but her father was very loath to take in his daughter, she had been so long away; but the mother said—"Truly she is ours; we will also take her deliverer in, for what he has done for our child. We will allow them to live together. She is baptised, and he is willing to be baptised into our faith." He was therefore baptised, and received a place called Abbey's Land, now Knapple Lands. He had to go three days every week to grind wheat for the castle, for the use of Lord Neish. The Abbot finding it hard work to drive the stone mill, he invented a mill to go by water, which was called Millnab, or the Abbot's Mill, west of Crieff, the first water mill of which we read in Britain. The M'Nabs grew into a great and numerous clan. Lord Neish seeing that they were descendents of the Romans, and being near the clan Cattan of the Forest, there were great disputes fell between the clans, he therefore sent them to his forests in Glendochart, and they had their possessions there. They married with the M'Larens and M'Alpins, who were their neighbouring clans.

ANCIENT HISTORY OF CALEDONIA. 93

A dispute having fallen out in England between the English and the Romans, several came back, saying that they were the real heirs of certain lands. Roger de Gomarie, a priest of the Church of Rome, came to claim Comrie Castle. Cattan, from Wales, claimed the Forest, now Auchterarder, as one of the ancient clan Cattan ; many more came back after they had learned a craft in the Romish Church, to try and get themselves settled. But none were believed, so they had to return back to the Romish Church without having their claims granted.

Few years elapsed when the clans got strong, but the Fenians waxed still stronger. They occupied the Fintry Hills, near to Campsie, and all that district they claimed as their own, and made many terrible butcheries of the king's loyal subjects, murdering M'Kenrick and all his clan, and bringing the country under tribute to the Church of Rome. King David was a wise and prudent king, as well as gallant and brave, so he suffered with them for a season, for at this time the Normans broke in under cloud of night and murdered all the Erskines of Skye, except a few whom they carried along with them. The king determined to punish them first, and allow the Fenians to go at liberty for a time. The beacon was once more placed on the Ringhead (Kinfauns,) and the banners of the M'Donalds were flying on the royal palace. All the M'Donalds of Morven, Glengarry, and Glencoe, the M'Phees of Fort William, the Stewarts of Appin, the M'Intyres, the Raiths, and Saint Laurence of Laurence, were all in readiness for the royal summons for war. The M'Kays were immediately ordered to be in readiness at the shortest notice, as they were the only clan who had boats to ferry the men over, for the crafty Normans kept all their boats in the isle. There were a great many Irish as well as Romans among them, with a leader named O'Diarmid. They had the flag of the Normans, but were still the same as the Fenians. The clan M'Kay were commanded by the chief's eldest son, James M'Kay. During the darkness of night, he took some of his faithful followers, and went and cut loose the boats belonging to the Danes, who murdered the people of the isle, and fetched them to the shore to be ready for the clans the following morning. The clans landed in the face of the Norman swords, as it was quite contrary to the Chaldean faith to draw a sword before sunrise. When the king's army had all got ashore, O'Diarmid fled back from the Normans, trying to make the apology of being forced. The wise king David, seeing that there were many islands around, asked them to depart to them, and cautioned them never to do the same again. Whilst offering that treaty to them, a villain of the Church of Rome tried to take the king's life, by thrusting at him with his copper dagger, but it did not touch the person of the king, as it never pierced the coat of mail which he wore. The king's attendants then cut the treacherous priest to pieces, and gallantly defended themselves until assistance reached them. This was the beginning of the battle of Erskine's Plains. The battle raged furiously, and no quarter was given on either side. Copper, brass, or tin had no share against the broadswords, which were made of the best steel. During the hottest of the battle, O'Diarmid thought to play some treachery upon David, and went to see if he could get the boats away, but found himself disappointed, because David had a strong party keeping the boats afloat, ready for his retreat if required. O'Diarmid and his Irish party seeing that those who fought least were safest, and not being able to get possession of the boats of his enemies, went and laid hold of those of his friends, and all the scattered boats which James M'Kay had not noticed in the dark. He embarked for the Irish shores, leaving the Normans to the mercy of the clans. The Norman army by noon was nearly cut up, and throwing down their swords they awaited their fate. But Donald said it was nothing less than murder to slay unarmed men. Couran, the chief leader of the Normans, seeing that there was mercy to be got from king David, promised to quit the isle, and all the isles which belonged to the Caledonians, and to put an end to the buildings at Shetland, and deliver it into the hands of the Caledonians. The king allowed him to stay six months on the island to recover his army.

The island was offered to Erskine of Mar, but he refused to take it, saying—" Are you to rob the infant daughter of my murdered kinsman? I thought I was fighting for a true and just king; never did I suppose that you would rob the fatherless." He then turned away in wrath. The king was dismayed, seeing that Erskine was a branch of a powerful clan, a true branch of the blood of Saint Laurence of Dundee. M'Donald of Morven, cousin to the king, said—" Ye know not what he meaneth." " What is it ?" asked David. He answered—" There is a child of the murdered Erskine who was in my house at Morven, when my sister along with her husband was murdered, and still resides with me." The king sent a messenger to the camp of the M'Larens, where Erskine was taking counsel with his kinsmen as to the king's attempt to defraud an orphan of her claim. The messenger requested Erskine to go to the king. Erskine immediately put on his armour, with sword and dagger, and went. David arose from his seat with a smile, saying—" Why are you thus equipped ?" He returned—" I always go in armour to talk to an enemy." " I am not your enemy," replied the king, " and hope never I will be." Erskine replied—" He who hath no justice in his heart is my most deadly enemy." David returned—" I swear by the crown of King Kenneth, which I am allowed to wear, the crown of your forefather, that I never knew the murdered Erskine had a child alive. I would be the last who would defraud the least in my dominions of anything granted them by the will of God. Allow the child to remain with her mother's people, or take her to any chief's house of her own clan, and when she shall come of age, and is taught the rules of the Church by the saints, and baptised, then let her choose any one from the loyal clans to be ruler of her father's lands and chief of that clan." She grew, and chose Donald M'Donald, the chief of Morven, but he gave it up to his second brother. Her descendants were chiefs of the M'Donalds, and finished Slate Castle, most of which was built by the Picts, while the Normans were in possession of the Isles. She was the mother of two twin brothers, M'Leod the firstborn, and M'Lean the younger. M'Leod got a place called Dunveighan. M'Lean, going about doing nothing, grew up to manhood, having no land, sometimes in Morven, sometimes in Skye. A house was built for the eldest. The youngest was grieved to see his brother receiving so much preference ; and it is wrote in some part of the castle, and still preserved—" M'Lean shall not be out, and M'Leod in." M'Lean was a strong muscular man, and went about watching the motions of all the clans. One day he said to his father —"I see an island which is still possessed by lawless people, calling their leader O'Moulon. They carry off the cattle from the Borders, and disturb the country very much. Give me your banner, and the M'Larens with the M'Donalds will rise with me to destroy that robber." He roused the M'Phees, the M'Larens, the Comries of Comrie Castle, the M'Duffs, the M'Inroys, the M'Larens of Lawers, the Erskines, and the Kennedys, and went to the king for liberty to attack O'Moulon. The king gave them every encouragement, and ordered a part of every branch of the M'Donalds, the M·Kays, the Cattans, the Waldenses of Gleneagles, the Colvilles and Melvilles of Fife, the Condochies, and the Robertsons to be mustered. They marched with Saint Fillans, the chief of the Blythes, at their front. They had no boats to land their men. There were boats at Skye, but they were always kept on duty, for fear of an invasion as before. The army not being numerous, only a few out of each clan, they lodged with their relations. O'Moulon's plundering party came ashore, when the M'Phees with the M'Intyres captured the boats, and slew every man of them, allowing none of them to escape to carry the news back. They then hid the boats near to the spot, knowing that ere long some other boats would be sent after them; and after a few nights' watching, a boat landed with a harper professing to be blind, with a boy leading him. " What news ?" cried he, in his broken Irish language. They answered—" None, except you have got some." He passed through the country playing his harp, and seeing no disturbance or appearance of any army, he, to draw the people, said there was a great army of Normans coming among them. They answered—" Deal that among yourselves; you put up with it best." He then departed with his boat, and went to O'Moulon, and told him the news. O'Moulon ordered three times the number of the former band to be sent, so that they could fight a good battle, and take a good booty, expecting to have only to fight with the clan M'Intyre, who were upon the Borders, possessing

Argyleshire. M'Alpin was immediately despatched for the M'Gregors, thinking that the force would be too great for them. David of Scone told them that only a part of the M'Alpins and none of the Grahams were allowed to go for fear of a plot by the Irish and Normans. Accordingly, O'Moulon, the king of Mull, attacked the country with a strong party of robbers, knowing that the clans had no boats to pursue them. When all had left the shore, except those left to guard the boats, M'Phee and M'Alpin, and part of the M'Intyres, fell upon a plan to deceive the boatmen unless they might fly to sea with them. They had the cattle gathered to one spot, and whilst the robbers were ranging the country, the clansmen loosed the cattle, and came with a number of them towards the boats. Beside every cow a clansman crept carefully; while the M'Phees, being acquainted with boats, sprang instantly into the boats, M'Lean at the lead, and brandishing his sword cried—" The boats are ours." The poor dismayed boatmen had to fly into an enemy's country. Immediately the sound of the pibroch, with beacons blazing, aroused every clan to their banners, and manning the boats they passed over to the shores of Mull, where a battle ensued between the clans and the king's army. M'Lean declared his right to the island, but they insisted that it was theirs, as it was nearer the coasts of Ireland than Caledonia. M'Lean proved that it was not, and the furious chief of the M'Intyres cried—" What is the use of this wrangling ? He must either give up his claim, or fight for it." O'Moulon asked three days to consider, as he thought that by that time his men would be returned, as well as assistance from the neighbouring isles, as they were all inhabited by Fenians or such like rebels. M'Lean offered to fight for it single-handed, so that no other blood might be spilt, the one who overcame to get the island. The king refused, declaring that he held it by the authority of the Holy Father, the Pope of Rome, and the Cardinal of Iona. M'Lean made reply— " Neither you, the Pope, nor the Cardinal, have a right to these islands." O'Moulon seeing that the clans were not near his number, and that another fleet was coming to his aid from the shore, and being so sure of victory, from the meagre number of the clans, sent a party to capture their boats to make sure that he would slay them all, and that none would escape. A great battle then ensued, chiefly by the Rivens. The battle was terrible but short. They attacked the king and his army on the beach, and shortly after the battle was finished. O'Moulon fled to see what was come of the fleet which was approaching, but found that they were likewise clansmen. He then drowned himself in a place called Moulon's Pool. The clans then gave the remainder of the Fenians some spare boats to leave for the Irish coast, allowing them six days to quit the island, and any found after the expiry of that time were to be put to death. M'Lean built his house at a place called Loch Bowie or the Yellow Lake, and being married to the sister of the chief of the Rivens, became the founder of the M'Leans. M'Phee and his fleet went and freed all the Western Islands. M'Alpin got Isla; M'Phee got the island of Colsey, being the furthest out island to the south-west belonging to Caledonia; the son of Comrie got Comrie Island. The clans were thus placed through the islands with great fleets of boats, and settled themselves there as true and loyal subjects. Iona was left alone for the time. Alpin was married to a daughter of the chief of the M'Intyres of Kintyre.

The Western Islands were now perfectly free, but king David at Scone was very much grieved by the cruel murders committed upon his loyal subjects everywhere by the Fenians, who claimed all south of the Forth as their own, being greatly mixed with Scotts. The Druids of Wales, who were under the character of Gipsies, broke out and murdered Cardin, Drummond, and Gartmore, the cruel monsters killing the helpless women and children, crying— "To h—— with you and your children! Why did you not flee to the mountains?" The king was by these acts of cruelty goaded to madness, and every banner was again hoisted. The king's banner was carried by M'Kay of Kelty, who was called the king's bannerman. David, during the peace, had procured a fleet of boats; and instead of his usual way of stemming the streams, he had his boats prepared to carry them across, every boatman having a piece of land for attending upon the boats to ferry over all his loyal subjects. Even to the King's Cairn, on the Forth, there were boats prepared for passage, with one furlong of land for men and cattle, clear of all king's duties. The boatmen upon the Forth were sworn not to sleep one night with their boats on the south side, for fear of the Fenians taking advantage of them. The Fenians entered Dumbarton, and killed many of the clans Lennox and Saint Parlin, and committed the College to flames, many of the people of Dumbarton shutting themselves up in the castle for safety. Frune, who was a usurper, killed Saint Parlin at Bannocher Castle, and claimed the country, placing his brother Phene at a place called Glenfruin. This enraged every clan, as they all had some relation or friend murdered. The blood of the Grahams of Montrose boiled at the murder of Graham of Gartmore, and the M'Gregors and M'Alpins for the murder of Cardin and Drummond, who were M'Gregors. The deaths of Strathenricks (M'Endrick in the Highlands, and Henderson in the Lowlands), a branch of the M'Gregors, were never revenged. They nearly occupied all Saint Arthur's Plains, now called Monteath. The people fled to Saint Arthur's Monastery, which is to be seen to this day. They even attacked the Forests of Balquhidder, but M'Inroy, a forester of the M'Laren clan, who had observed the motions of the Fenians, alarmed the clachan town of Saint M'Isaac, now called Callander of Monteath, and the people fled to the mountains, and escaped the wrath of the Fenians, who boasted that they would do what no nation could do before. They then attacked the passes where often before the Romans had been defeated. At this time a messenger arrived at Balquhidder, ordering forward the four Barons with all their clans to Scone Palace; but the answer was given by Riven of Atnample, a descendant of the M'Larens, saying—" We have been engaged disputing the pass with the Fenians." The king hearing of this, hastened with all his force to the frontier. The Fenians retreated, thinking that by some cunning plan they would slaughter the king's army at night. They fled back across the ground which they had gained, carrying great booty with them. Clery, a crafty Irishman, fled with his party beyond a bog, thinking the king's army would instantly follow him. But the Arthurs, knowing the ground too well, said—" Follow them not, it is a dangerous swamp. Let them alone ; they have no provisions, and cannot stir in any direction, as the swamp is a floating moss. He has only one spot upon which he can go, which is called the Maw's Island." The clans immediately commenced cutting branches from the trees with their Lochaber axes and other weapons, and laid them on the moss, and put up the hides of bulls on large poles in front of their camp, which rendered Clery's bowmen of no use, as the arrows could not penetrate through the cattle hides. The clans got within cross-bow range, and the king ordered none to go forward but mountain foresters of every clan, to cut holes with their skeen dhus, so that they might get the points of their arrows through. Every forester had twenty-four Fenians' lives depending upon him, as he carried twenty-four arrows in his belt, and made sure that each one would cause the death of a Fenian. Clery saw no other chance of escape except to try the swamp again, where many of his men were drowned. Clery then sent a Caledonian whom he had captured to king David as an ambassador, informing him that he would give himself up on condition that he would grant him his life and his men's lives, when he would depart from his dominions. The king answered—"Deceive yourself not, because the first gallows tree will bear thy body, with a piece of bull-hide round thy neck, as also the last man of your midnight murderers." The slave was not allowed to go back, but an armed man clad in armour went half way and told them the king's message. Clery then made another determined attempt to cross the Black River, now called the Forth, to make for the south, but he and all his army disappeared. A strict examination was made after a few days by the king's orders, to see if there was any appearance of life, but it was found that they were all dead. The king carefully watched for any fugitives who might have escaped, and examining the house of Gartmore, he found that the nurse during the murder had fled into the cellar with her young charge, the young Graham. She had taken care of the child, along with a pet goat for which he had a great liking. At night she went out for food to the goat, and lay all day in the dark and dreary cellar, having no other food than the goat's milk until she was relieved by her rescuers. She was carefully taken to an island where there was a church of Saint Arthur, where all the unprotected who had escaped were placed.

David seeing that the Fenians had a great army collected out of all nations, having no flag, but going about committing all sorts of cruelty and murder, and he being now pretty far advanced in years, and not very fit to command an army, he gave the whole charge of the war to his son Donald, under the charge of Kenneth M'Alpine of Duplin. They had to remain a few days for the Western Highlanders to join them with Donald M'Donald, Prince M'Alpin of Isla, and Saint Laurence of Laurence, as leaders. They intended to relieve Dumbarton Castle immediately; but Buchanan of Buchan seeing that he was not in a very agreeable situation, came to King Donald with his wife and all his family, from the Fenian camp, and throwing down their arms, declared themselves innocent of any of the murders. By their own desire they were admitted into the Church, and joined to the M'Gregors. Buchanan and his wife, being old people, were allowed to go back to their home, but their sons were enlisted into the royal army to fight along with the M'Gregors. The furious Douglas wished to advance instantly upon his southern enemy, but the rulers wished to draw them out from their mountains, to ascertain their number and know what opposition they might expect, for they occupied the Fintry Hills, or the Fenians' Hills. About midnight, the Fenians, being best acquainted with the country, made an attack upon a party who were outside the camp cooking, but they fled with all speed into the camp and aroused the clans. Little was done that night, as the Fenians fled as soon as they saw that the clans were on the alert. Next morning the clans observed a strong body of the Fenian army encamped at a place called Strathblane, under the command of four leaders, Fruin, Gare, Blania, and Loman, all four being usurpers and rate takers. The armies then advanced from both sides with rapidity, and the battle commenced. The Fenians were reinforced from other quarters; but although the clans were all along the smaller body, they still kept their ground. Blania fell in a hand-to-hand fight with the Douglas. The battle went in favour of Douglas, although the Fenians were two to one. At this time Saint M'Laren, being singled out, was rushed upon by a Fenian and slain, and the place was called Killearn. The men, because he was a preacher of the Gospel, cried out—" Alas! what shall we do ?" His son, bursting forward, cried—" Foolish men, does the Lord not know best what to do with his own ?" The king observing the young M'Laren's valour, said—" The hawk's flight or the hound's hunt shall be yours." The second son, named John, came forward in rage at seeing his father lying breathless on the ground, and rushed upon the enemy, joined by the M'Phees of Lochaber and the Comries, both being branches of his own clan. They rushed so headlong into the battle that they were almost past all control. The Fenians began to fly for the mountains. Loman retreated southward. The second son of M'Laren with his party pursued them, and made a great many prisoners. The Fenians seeing that they were nearly overtaken by the light-footed clansmen, fled into a marsh or bog, seeing that the horsemen belonging to Comrie were close upon them. The king being afraid that their young leader would rush into danger, despatched a party of Douglas' horsemen to his aid. By this time the young heroic M'Laren cried—" Dismount, spear in hand." He was immediately obeyed, when a great number of the Fenians seeing that they were perfectly overpowered, cried out for mercy. The M'Laren returned—" You ask mercy to murder us; was ever such demand heard ?" A great number surrendered, thinking that they would yet receive their requests. The M'Laren kept his word, and gave every man who hung an hundred his liberty with a mark which would keep him out of all danger. After executing his design, he returned to the king, who said—" You have played your part well. You shall receive the spot whereon you gained your victory, and your name shall be Spear-in-hand." The name of the spot is the Fenians' Tree, or Fintry. The spot where M'Laren built his house was called Killcrioch, or the Gallows Burying Ground. He was the founder of the Spears in Scotland. The M'Kays and M'Donalds had joined and pursued Loman's party with the M'Intyres; but in the afternoon the Fenians being strengthened, the clans had to fall back with great loss. Donald himself was severely wounded, and one of the Douglases was slain. A council of war was appointed, when it was thought expedient to call the Lennox and M'Farlane clans, and it was found that Feen with all his party had been engaged in the battle, he being brother to Fruin. The clans Lennox and M'Farlane came to their assistance, the two armies lying in sight of one another. The clan Cattan and the Neishes sent as many as they could to strengthen the king's army; but the old king David, fearing an invasion from the Danes, ordered that not one man north of the Earn was to be taken to the battle. The council having advised the renewal of the fight, M'Kay of the Law with his party went to a hill top to surprise Loman's rear, whilst the king from his wounds had to be carried back to the rear of his army, to the house of Fruin, the Fenian leader, which he had lately deserted. The battle was then conducted by the Douglas, Kenneth M'Alpin of Duplin, the Prince of the Isle, and M'Laren of Lourn. Loman finding that the clans were still for war, fled back some distance for the sake of more ground; but he soon found that the rising ground which he intended to have occupied was already in the possession of the M'Kays, and finding his communication cut off, and not knowing the number of the M'Kays, he sent some of the wounded prisoners from the former day's fight, offering to deliver up all his prisoners and depart beyond the Clyde with all his people. The four leaders having consulted, every piper was ordered to play the advance, which they did from the hill called Millgie, or David's Hill, which was afterwards granted to a man called "Dun Davie," one of the M'Kays, the founder of the Duns of Strathblane. The battle being resumed, the M'Kays did great execution in Loman's army with their bowmen, by sending showers of arrows amongst his men. He only escaped with a few of his nobles, all the rest being slain. They fled towards a ford which they were acquainted with on the Clyde. Being closely pursued there, they cried—"Give in, give in;" but the clans not knowing what they meant, abated none. The place was called "Givin Ford," or Gavin. The Fenians then came to a marsh when their leader cried "Rin through." The place is now called Renfrew. The clans then returned to look after their wounded and slain. It was agreed that those who had most distinguished themselves should get lands. The Baron of Lourn was made Baron of Glasgow, and the "Grey Dog's Hunt." This is the town of which Saint M'Isaac in his prophecy spoke as "The Grey Dog's Town." The oldest son of the slain M'Laren, and brother of John the Spear-in-hand, was created Baron of Lourn. A council of war was afterwards held at Broom Haugh, near the Clyde, now called the Broomielaw. It was thought proper to suspend the war for a season, after posting strong guards, as the king was dangerously ill. This is believed to be about the sixth or seventh century.

They began to build a Chaldean Church at Glasgow, for the doctrine of Christ. There had been a good number of huts where people had resorted to, since the Roman invasion, but they were now completely deserted, the people having fled to the south with the Fenians. The Earl of Glasgow required to be supported by the clans to keep his new possessions against an enemy. The clans thereafter dispersed to their separate homes, lamenting their dead and wounded. For a whole season afterwards there was no war, except some plundering excursions. The prince of Montrose sent a company of Grahams to protect the young heir of Gartmore, and each clan supported the other, as they were required ; for the Fenians could not content themselves, but must always be making inroads upon some clan. David died about 680 A.D., and was succeeded by Donald his son. Kenneth M'Alpin of Duplin was appointed Regent, seeing that the young king, from sorrow for the death of his father, and his wounds, was unable to rule the nation. The Regent next season gathered all the clans of Caledonia, and marched towards the west, when he gave pieces of land to every one who followed him beyond the Clyde. They went to clear the land of all rebels, and they advanced beyond the Clyde without ever drawing a sword. Loman declared that this part of the country was their fathers' share, and that he would dispute it to the last. Near to Killwinning, Loman with his Fenian band drew up in line of battle, but immediately the clans extended their lines, determined to meet the foe. King Kenneth wished a little delay, as he had despatched an order for the Western Highlanders to land beyond the Clyde; but the prince of the Western Isles, along with the M'Kays, were ordered to remain at home for fear of the Danish invasion which was expected. The M'Intyres, the M'Alpins, and M'Larens, were the three clans sent to the south. The clans were well provided with provisions, so that they could rest in sight of the enemy for a long time. The intention of the Fenians was to attack the camp under cover of night; but the watchful eye of M'Alpin, who was son-in-law to the king, was on the alert, and seeing the attack about to be made, he immediately sounded the advance by the pibroch. M'Alpin then addressed them, expressing the hope that every man would do his best in the absence of their king. The battle commenced furiously; but though the Fenians were fully double the number of the clansmen, they found themselves unable to cope with the broadswords. Comrie and Douglas advanced on horseback with long spears, and hewed down the Fenians, who had only swords made from copper and brass. The Fenians seeing the day was lost, fled towards the west. Douglas and Comrie pursued them too far, and were surrounded by the flying enemy. A terrible engagement then commenced between them and the overwhelming Fenians. The Regent immediately ordered an advance of infantry to save the horse, and he had to fall back with a heavy loss in order to allow assistance to be sent to them, but he held his ground good near to Camlich. He fortified himself there for a few days, and held a council of war to see what could next be done. The Baron of Glasgow and David of Millgie, considered that if the Fenians gained one victory there would be no living with them, so they agreed to hold their situation good for the present, until they could send for M'Duff and the clans of Fife, with part of the Blythes; but Saint Fillans, the chief of the Blythes, said that the sea robbers were so plenty that it was not known when nor where they might break in. During these debates they noticed a great increase in Loman's army. King Kenneth ordered every man to dismount from his horse, and to fight upon foot, on account of the rugged grounds. His orders received instant obedience. The horses were sent back amongst the cattle in the rear, under the protection of a strong body for guarding the cattle from the Fenians. At night, whilst every man was watching at his post, they espied a lame beggar, who expressed a wish to see M'Alpin himself, and told him that Kenny, the son of Kenneth of Isla, was come. M'Alpin asked the man what number Kenny had with him, and the beggar returned that he had all the M'Intyres, M'Leans, the Comries of Comrie's Isle, the M'Larens of Lourn, and a good many of the Stewarts of Appin, and the M'Phees of Collessie. The beggar was then sent to Kenny, to tell him that the clans were to advance by break of day, and instructing him to advance during the night as near to the Fenians as possible. Early next morning, the king led forward his army as leader of the M'Alpins, the M'Donalds being led by a kinsman of King Donald. They made a heavy charge upon the Fenians, and Kenny of Isla then attacked the rear of the Fenian camp. The battle went on until about high noon, when Lennox of Dumbarton came up with a great band and fell upon the right wing of the Fenians. Loman, who was at a good distance with his rulers, fled from the field, leading off in the direction of Berwick, which was infested with lawless bands. The clans then cleared the country of that band of robbers, even to the Solway Firth, and then ordered them to go beyond the Tweed. They made answer that they would not, as they were the Scottish nation, although their king had run away to the Caledonians; but the king began to divide the land beyond the Clyde, according to his promise. He gave Donald M'Donald, who led part of the army, a place called Dundonald; he gave Comrie, the second son of Comrie of Comrie Castle, the "Eagle's flight," now called Eagleton; the second son of M'Intyre received a place called Tyrebolton; the son of king Kenneth of Isla received a place called Kenniscomed; Saint Lennox's son received a place called Saint Lennox Land, or Largs; Nathiel received a place called Neithsdale; the Grahams received a place called Netherby; the Johnstons got back their own possessions in Annandale; one of the M'Gregors, who was married to the daughter of Saint Michael, who was murdered by the Fenians, received her father's possessions at Dumfries, and was the founder of the Gregorsons or

Greigs; and all those who had formerly held possessions there received back their own. During the persecution by the Romans many had fled to Wales and France, but now returned. The sons of Lizzie came back, under the name of Lindsay, and the sons of Helen, under the name of Elliots, and each got the lands of his mother. Ancient Caledonia was again in possession of her own people, but the Scots were still in a rebellious state, and kept the country in a very troubled condition.

There came a great famine across the Scottish nation, and they took to their old trade of robbery. King Donald sent a message to the kings of England that if they claimed the Scottish nation, they must control it. The answer from some of the kings was that when King Donald paid homage to the Pope they would give him an answer. When the king heard this, he said—" We must deal with bad neighbours as best as we can, for this is not a wholesome warfare." The Caledonians remained contented, and defended themselves as best they could.

The king, hearing that the boatmen whom his father had placed with lands and the boats made by the Waldenses to ferry all his men and cattle across the river, were levying charges upon passengers, he disguised himself at a place called Inver, whilst going to visit his forest and hunting-tower at Logierait. Here the boatman demanded a bodle, a small copper coin about the value of half a farthing. The king said—" Did not the good king David give you or your father land, house, and boat, to serve his loyal subjects free of all expense? You must ferry over every man who has the badge of his clan in his bonnet, but not those who are outlaws and have no badge." The boatman, perceiving that he was dealing with some royal personage, fell upon his knees, crying—" It was not I, but Kate my wife who proposed it." The king replied—" If you exact a bodle from any of my loyal subjects, both Kate and you will be hung upon yon tree where you fasten your boat, until your bones be bleached as white as my shirt." The boatman went home cursing her for her greed, which had put their necks in danger. The boat's rest throughout all Caledonia was one furlong square upon both sides of the river. The three lengths of the king's tilting spear beyond the waves was free ground for all loyal subjects.

The king went to Logierait and died there. The Baron of Dundonald claimed the crown from the race of the M'Donalds, but the nation loved the regent king, Kenneth M'Alpin. But as he was pretty old, he told them that they might do as they thought fit, but he was of opinion that the sister's son of the deceased king had more right to the crown than a kinsman as far back as third cousin. But he left it with the nation to do as they thought proper. Every clan was ordered to send forward five men to nominate a king. They all assembled before the palace at Scone. Those for M'Alpin were to turn to the right, and those for Dundonald were to turn to the left. Young Kenneth was chosen by a great majority, and was crowned after the usual form, under the name of king Kenneth M'Alpin the Second, by the saints of the Chaldean faith, being seated on the marble chair, with his feet resting on Jacob's Pillow. He was advised by his father to leave the Scottish nation alone, as they were so unruly. He had a quiet, peaceable reign, the clans occupying their time with sports and amusements of every description, while laws and religion flourished.

The Britons and all who paid homage to the Church of Rome claimed to put priests and bishops into all the old churches which were said to have been built by the Picts, but were denied by the Caledonian king, who said—" Let the Scots do as they please in their own country. There was a union formed between Caledonia and Scotland, but they neither assist us nor yet do they pay us homage." The Pope was displeased at this reply from a stripling king, whom he said he would soon make to lie down in Rome until he should tread upon his neck. He immediately ordered a fleet to proceed against that lawless country, and not having the caution of some other popes, sent also a great many Waldenses, who had been captured for their religion. The Waldenses knew that they were going to their friends' country; and as soon as they landed on the west coast, they, along with a great many French who had been forced into the war, fled and joined the Caledonian army. This gave king Kenneth great encouragement, and so greatly enriched Caledonia with arms, money, and men, that they demanded the subjection of the Scots, according to the first union. King Kenneth then gathered his army, giving honour to the old heroes' sons who had been in the field before, and especially to the Baron of Dundonald, M'Donald of Badenoch, Angus M'Donald of Brechin, and Prince M'Donald of the Isles, as these were all connected with the royal family. Marching to the south, with the third man of every clan, he reached Dunfermline, which was a royal residence. Crossing the Forth in the king's boats, he embodied his whole army at a place called Towerwood, near Falkirk, and marching to a place which was built by the Picts and Scots, he ordered one of the Scots who was in possession to quit his palace and raise his clan to join his banner, or prepare for battle. For creeds, he allowed such to be settled according as conscience dictated, but he claimed all rights and lands. The Pope and prelates gathered a large army, declaring that victory would follow them wherever they went against the Caledonians, who were heretics, and that the Pope would destroy the last Caledonian. The Pope's army drew up west from Edinburgh, and King Kenneth was advised by his warriors to withdraw to the rising ground. This great battle was fought with great cruelty on both sides. During the fight, the young king and Douglas coming in contact, the one almost slew the other by mistake, both having got the plumes cut from their helmets, ere they recognised each other. The priests and prelates began to fly from the field when they saw what dreadful havoc was going upon both sides. During the night the clans gathered their dead and wounded, whilst some women were going through the field looking for their own. Early next morning, the king said to Douglas—" You fought well." Douglas answered—" What should I have been doing when my noble king was so busy?" The king said to Douglas—" Get me a saint with parchment." The saint afterwards came and said of Douglas—" Go view these plains; they are all yours, and more towns than that." He was then called the Baron of Moreton. The king went with armed men, and demanded the keys of Edinburgh, but an abbot answered him that they would not be given up, as they would very soon be relieved by an army from the holy Pope. The king put off no time with him, but pursued after an army which was flying to the south. A great number of them shut themselves into a monastery called Roselin. The king's army having greatly increased, he allowed the Scots north of the Tweed forty days to acknowledge him as the crowned king of Scotland as well as Caledonia. They submitted and paid homage. The king did not interfere with their creed, but they had to join his banner, as he could not trust them to remain at home.

About this time the Britons made a movement, by order of the Pope, to march against the rebel king of Caledonia, and all who denied the faith of Rome. They crossed the Tweed at a place called Coldstream. Kenneth called a council of war at a place called Greenlaw, desiring all who had joined his army recently to return back if they did not wish to draw weapons against their creed; but those who went were to have no claim to lands in Scotland or Caledonia. The well-known flag of the king of Britain (the red dragon) was hoisted, and then the green pine tree branch, with the bloody hand of the M'Donalds, and the red lion, went up. The pibrochs of every clan blew out the advance. The king cried to Saint Johnstone, his chaplain on the field—"Stay back and pray for us." The saint, taking this as an insult, being a little behind, sprang to the front and cried—"Every man can pray for himself. I can fight my own share." The battle then commenced, and when night closed upon the dreadful day both companies had to withdraw. The king of Caledonia drew his army off the field to some hard ground where his cavalry might be of some use. The commander of the ancient Britons carefully sought the pass where he had crossed the former day, but unfortunately for him, the Tweed had overflown its banks. Next day the two armies lay in sight of one another without drawing a sword, each collecting their wounded. The commander of the Britons sent to the king of the Caledonians an ambassador who had once been in Caledonia before, informing him that he would retire from his borders upon the condition that he would release all the prisoners who were confined in the castles. The king called a council of what he had alive of his nobles, as many of them were slain, and Saint Johnstone said unto the ambassador, by the king's commands—" We came not here to make conditions, we came to fight a battle ; but deliver up all that are of our creed in your camp, and you may remain on our borders until the river admit of your retreat." Loudon and Lauder, two Welsh leaders who had been forced from their own country, and were true followers of the creed according to the preaching of the apostles, came to the king of Caledonia and paid him homage. Seeing that their race were numerous, the king gave them the lands of Loudon and Lauderdale amongst the Scots, to be a check against any rebellion again taking place. The king told Saint Johnston of John's Town to write out the grant. Saint Johnstone said he had no pen. The king replied—" Take a pen out of that cock ;" and the place, near Roselin, is called Cockpen to this day. He opened all the city gates, and allowed all the priests and prelates who had shut themselves up to walk away unmolested, and then returned north of the Forth ; and seeing that Scone palace was too far out of his way, and that Edinburgh was too near his enemy, he caused the royal residence to be at Dunfermline. Everything prospered under his reign, which reached almost to the eight hundredth year after Christ. He built a large boat which crossed every week, and fetched across the Gaberlunzie men, who went about gathering news through the country, the first substitute for newspapers. The Baron of Moreton, the heroic Douglas, ruled as king all south of the Firth. All tributes and king's dues were paid to him. But the Pope could not remain at rest. The Waldenses still professed Christianity perfectly opposite to the rules of the Pope, and commenced to trade with Caledonia ; and during the persecution, a great number fled into Holland, which was famous for its religion, being inhabited by Christians from Jerusalem and all parts of the world, who had fled from their persecutors. The Pope followed them even into Holland with a great persecution, and many of the Waldenses and French came over to Scotland, thereby enriching it with all kinds of armour and other goods which they could bring in ships. The Pope seeing from past experience that Caledonia was fully his match, did not interfere with it.

Berwick became one of the greatest manufacturing towns in Britain, being even larger than London at that date, and far surpassing Edinburgh. It also made great advances in learning, being the first place where the English and French languages were written. The country remained quiet during the latter part of the king's reign, with no disturbance worth placing upon the history of the country.

King Kenneth II. died at Dunfermline, and leaving no son to fill his vacant throne, the crown was disputed by M'Alpin of Duplin, M'Alpin of Breadalbane, M'Alpin of Isla, and Kenneth M'Alpin of Cunningham, all branches of the family of Dunalpin, now called Duplin. The dispute was so great that it was like to put the nation into civil war; but the old barons of the ancient families, appointed the Baron of Moreton, the late king's councillor, as regent. It was then agreed to settle it by what they called the "Bonnets." Five men of every clan assembled in front of Scone Palace, and chose Donald M'Donald of Dundonald, who was the nearest relative whom they could trace to the ancient race of the kings of Forteviot. He was accordingly crowned at Scone Palace, about the beginning of the ninth century. The M'Alpins still refused to pay tribute to the king, but they were soon suppressed, all the other clans being loyal to the newly-elected king.

The country remained in quietness until the Britons made another determined attempt to regain Berwick, because of its prosperous state. The young king with his wise adviser, the heroic Douglas, Baron of Moreton, who was now pretty well advanced in years, and his sons, who were leaders, in command, soon gathered a large army, as every one of the Lauders and Loudens turned out to a man, and were equal in bravery to any of the clans. The Britons had made a breach upon Western Caledonia, near Carlisle. The Elliots, Lindsays, and the Johnstones of Annandale, with the Black Johnstones, so named from the colour of their hair, assisted by the Lennoxes, had kept the Britons in check for three days, until king Donald arrived with his army upon the Border. The Britons were encamped on the south side of a river near to Carlisle, their front line glancing so as to have the appearance of one solid breast of iron, with armour. The Ayrshire men exclaimed that they could never penetrate them. They were led by the king's brother, second son of Dundonald, who cursed them for cowards, and asked if they believed at all in the powerful hand of God. Throwing down his armour, coat, and vest, he cried—" Let men follow me, and cowards return home." Every clan immediately followed his example, and swam across the river. The battle then commenced, and the M'Gregors of Dumfries with a party of the M'Michaels closed on the rear of the Britons, so that retreat was almost impossible. Night closed in upon the dreadful fray. During the night the Britons fled beyond the River Eden, and were encamped a good way off, thinking the Caledonians would not follow them. The king gave orders for all old and infirm men to return home, and the army then stemmed the river, shoulder to shoulder. The Britons retreated, the horse of Douglas and Montgomery following hard upon their rear. In their front was the river, and the horsemen were behind them. During the night they crossed that river, offering no battle or opposition to their pursuers, and were next morning followed by the Caledonians in the same mode. They pursued them thus even to the Castle of York; and a great extent of English land was given to Scottish nobles. The Scots claimed the whole lands to York for their own nation. This the king of Briton allowed them to have, and also to pay homage to their own king. He delivered up Northumberland, Cumberland, and Westmoreland, and part of Yorkshire along with its castle, saying—" If you get anything from these quarters it is more than ever I got." This settled the war, and the two kings with their followers returned to their respective boundaries.

But the Britons were not satisfied, and employed a nation called the Saxons to come to their assistance. The Saxons, under commanders of their own, marched to the north, claiming all the lands which the Britons had lost. In frantic rage they committed Berwick to the flames; and all the Border chiefs drove their cattle north, seeing that it was impossible to give battle to such a numerous and well-equipped army. Edinburgh was besieged, and forced to surrender for want of provisions, making laws and conditions. They then marched to the west, and encamped at a place near Airdrie, now called Monksland. All the clans that could be collected were encamped west of that. King Donald held a council of war to see whether he would surrender to their conditions or fight them. The Douglases all cried—" Better to have a dead man than a living coward." The Baron of Glasgow caught hold of the Bible in one hand and his sword in the other, and cried—" By these I live, and by these I'll die ;" then stepping in front of the M'Larens, he exclaimed—" Follow me." Immediately the king's flag was hoisted, the pibroch sounding the advance. The clans were completely defeated, and had to fly to the north. The Saxons killed the wounded who fell into their hands. King Donald ordered Stirling Castle to be stored with all kinds of provisions. After having so many of their chiefs slain, they thought it proper to go beyond the Forth, every clan joining in the march. The Saxons turned out all Chaldean saints, and if they did not quietly leave their churches, they were immediately put to a cruel death. The king returned back to Scone Palace, leaving the Saxons masters of all south of the Forth, on which they imposed heavy taxes. King Donald was married after his defeat to a daughter of Saint Laurence of Dundee, and contented himself within his small dominions with peace and pleasure. But the chiefs who had been put out of their possessions by the Southrons were very discontented, and those who remained amongst the Saxons were grievously burdened for money to the Church of Rome, and for the monks and friars at home ; and besides they had to send sheep and cattle to the Saxon camp, although they were starving themselves. The Saxons also took possession of all the best land in England. The Caledonian king, along with his nobles, watched for the first opportunity of freeing themselves from their tyrant. One of the Douglases, a harper, who could speak the Saxon language, went to see their number and condition, and the cause of their drawing so many of their army away, and forcing so many of the Scots to go with them. He very soon learned that a war had been begun between the Saxons and the Britons ; and having made certain that the Saxons were very thinly posted, and that they were forcing a great number of the Scots against their will to join in their war, he returned and told the king what he had learned. The king in less than one week had all the clans gathered around him, appointing two of the Douglases as commanders. James M'Laren, the son of Saint Laurence of Dundee, and M'Donald of Dundonald, who had been forced from his own ground, had commands likewise. With all their saints and rulers before them, they immediately marched across the Forth, as far south as Biggar. They then made an attack upon the Saxons. The Scots who had been compelled to lift arms, turned in the ranks upon the Saxons, and very nearly slew every Saxon themselves, as the Caledonian army never got a bow drawn, for fear of killing them. The Scots then joined their former king, Donald. The Saxons were defeated, and fled, leaving all they had behind. All monks, friars, and bishops, received only eight days to leave and go beyond the Tweed. The Saxons wanted them to treat with the friars, but they would not, stating that if they were not beyond the Tweed within the specified time they would all be hung upon the gallows tree. The king then pursued after the Saxons, with his army in two divisions. The Scots, rejoicing at being headed by their former king, pursued the Saxons with spirit, sparing no man who carried arms, until they reached the Tweed, which was the boundary agreed on in a treaty made before. The Scots, with a party of Frenchmen who had deserted from the Saxons, and a great many of the Waldenses, asked leave to follow the Saxons, to make them pay for the plunder which they had taken from Scotland and Wester Caledonia. The king held his council at a place called Greenlaw, near to the Border. His saints and rulers said—" It is better to have a small fire to warm us, than a big fire to burn us. We will be content with what we have got, and retain the Tweed as our boundary, as agreed upon by our fathers. Saint Johnstone of Saint John's Town told the king that the army was by far too large to remain together, provisions being scarce on the Border. It was therefore agreed that the Caledonian chiefs were to retire beyond the Forth, and to receive their ancient possessions, where they might live in peace and plenty. All churches were to be filled with priests of the Chaldean faith. The enraged Scots, along with the Gauls who had deserted the Saxons, and the Waldenses, headed by the valiant Douglas, and Davidson of Teviotsdale, crossed the Border after the king's return to Caledonia, and plundered the country all the way to Gloucester, the Saxons offering no opposition, with the exception of a few skirmishes. This plunder made the Border richer than at any former time in war and other instruments, and also in cattle and everything which England could produce. Lizzie's son, named Lindsay, was made Baron on the Border, and governor of Berwick. The whole of the Border chiefs were at this time anxious for war, goaded on by their former ravages and their late success; but none disturbed them, as the Saxons and Britons were at war at home.

The king, when returning to his ancient residence at Dunfermline, visited Erskine of Alloa, his kinsman, and appointed him ruler of the western division of Fife, giving orders that whatever monks or friars he might see were not to be touched in any manner, but were to be allowed to pass unmolested to their own country, as they had done great good in building churches and castles, and in introducing the art of writing, although in a strange language. But Erskine was very angry at this decree, as some of his kinsmen had been cruelly put to death by the monks. Saint Johnstone seeing the wrath of Erskine, passed the remark that we ought not to return evil for evil, but good for evil, upon which Erskine left the presence of the king, muttering something to himself. The king then returned with the Baron of Gowrie to Scone Palace, and established his court at Saint John's Town. He then issued an order to all churches to hold a day of fasting and prayer throughout all his dominions, for the great deliverance which they had had from the power of their would-be oppressors. The ancient Chaldean worship, with the administration of the Lord's Supper and Baptism, spread over all the dominions of the king, and the whole nation rested in peace for a considerable period.

A few years passed, when the king received a report from M'Duff, who was the ruler of the eastern district of Fife, that there were a great number of vessels arrived in the Forth, and a great many people were already landed, claiming to be the proper heirs to that place, as they were the founders of Saint Andrews, and that they were carrying off the cattle to their vessels. The king immediately fired his beacon at Ringhead, or Kinfauns, which soon gathered the clans and their chiefs to the scene of action. The M'Duffs, the Melvilles, the Blythes, the Colvilles, the Thomsons, and the M'Lours, kept the enemy in check. The Erskines had immediately repaired to their assistance, as they were the inhabitants of the western division of Fife. The king's army was in three divisions, so as to divide Fife from her surrounding enemies. They were led by St. Michael of Kirkmichael, who was both a warrior and a preacher. Finding that the robbers with their boats had gone up the water to the rocks of Pittenweem, they immediately followed, and had a heavy engagement on the plains of Balgona. After an obstinate encounter, the battle at last turned in favour of the Caledonians, and the plundering Danes and Normans had to fly to their boats. After the battle, the Douglas and Saint Michael were walking together, when a wounded Dane, who was lying on the path side, seeing the armour of Saint Michael partly open, thrust his spear through his body, and cried something in the Danish language, supposed to be that he had served his king to the last. So fell the gallant Saint Michael, and the place was called Killmichael. The Douglas was thus left chief commander of the army, though quite a young man. He grieved very much for the saint's death, as also for the commander of the Cameron clan, of whose death he heard next morning. He had died upon the field during the night, of the wounds received in the field. He was a brave and valiant man, and the spot was called Cameron's Tomb, now Cameron Bridge. Douglas and his army met the king at Melon's Hill, now called Melville Hill. The Camerons, who were only a new clan, this being one of their first engagements, were enraged beyond measure at the loss of their valiant commander, and were determined to have his death avenged. The king, turning to the Douglas, said—" The plains of Balgona are yours; and the best parish in Fife is to be given to the son of Cameron for the loss of his father. And both of you fall back, as you have fought valiantly already, being young men." The Douglas with the

Cameron were displeased with this command, and asked the king to allow them to engage, so that they might avenge the death of their friends. The king answered—"Such men as you two are few in my dominion, but do as God directs." The Douglas immediately advanced to the front of his scattered clans, and Cameron headed his men, crying to them to avenge the death of their chief. The advance was sounded from the right by the king, under the flag of the M'Donalds, and the flag of every clan was soon flying above the army. The Normans and Danes, fearing the attack which was about to be made, drew up a front for battle with spearsmen, but they were soon broken in upon by Montgomery's horse, followed by the heroic Douglas. The battle went on with fearful havoc, but the tin mail and the copper spears of the enemy were not equal to the hard iron of the Gows of Athole. Inster at last, seeing that they must yield, and that their escape was impossible, fled to his boat. His men, left thus to the mercy of the Caledonians, cried—"We are conquered; we are conquered." The Caledonians asked what they meant, and they sent over one Saint Menance as ambassador; but the king said—"Kill them all, and then they will be conquered." The place was called Killconquer. The place from where Inster fled and left his men to their fate was called after him. Those of the enemy who could get boats made their escape from the shores of Caledonia, leaving the two saints who had been pressed into their army, named Saint Menance and Saint Ninian, who formed the first union of Christianity between this country and Holland, which was often a refuge to our persecuted saints. They were both of the same belief as the Chaldeans with regard to Baptism and the Lord's Supper. Saint Menance built a church according to a foreign plan, which is to be seen to this day. Saint Ninian was a man of great learning, and went about visiting the colleges. He visited the college of Dull in its prosperous state, as it was the principal place of learning of the Chaldean saints of these days; and he formed a monastery out from Snowtown, or Stirling, which is called Saint Ninian's Church to this day. The well where he baptised at Dull is called Saint Ninian's Well. Religion spread very fast, as these two men brought the full Mosaic Law and a complete copy of the New Testament in Latin. Commerce commenced between this country and Holland, and the Waldenses.

The defeat of the Danes and Normans gave peace to Caledonia during the remainder of King Donald's reign, which allowed the people of Holland to come into this country and teach the people the art of fishing. Donald was succeeded by his son David, who was both prudent and wise. He went to the Border in disguise, as a great many complaints reached him from his Border chiefs against the people of Northumberland. He saw that there was more fault with his own people than their opponents, so he returned to Saint John's Town, and called his counsellors and passed a decree that no party more numerous than five men were to cross the Tweed. This enraged the Border chiefs very much, seeing that it put an end to all their acts of plunder; but it gave great satisfaction to all the other inhabitants upon the Border, and drew the love of all his subjects. He afterwards went to Holland to go through a course of learning, and was married to one of the royal family of Holland, who were of a very ancient race. She was called the good Queen Elizabeth. She taught young females the letters, and also sewing and all kinds of needlework, which was almost extinct for the want of practice. David enjoyed a quiet and peaceful reign. If he noticed the least appearance of any disturbance between his chiefs or people, he called a council of saints to put it down by the mildest means possible. He sent both arms and men to assist the persecuted Waldenses, who almost constantly suffered persecution, and many eminent preachers of the Gospel of Christ came from that quarter. As the whole writings of the New Testament were in the Latin language, and the Old Testament in the Hebrew, it was difficult for preachers to expound it to the people, as they had both to translate and study it. The king by this time was turning very old, so he counselled his son Donald, who was to be his successor, to be slow in wrath, and true and sure in judgment, and to be certain not to raise his word against those who preached the Gospel of Christ; to be always ready to defend his own, but never to be the cause of any quarrel, especially with any other power; to give no power of life or death to any except himself, without first consulting the Parliament. So died the wise and prudent king David, leaving his son Donald in his stead. This is the ancient history, as written by the king's chief priest.

Shortly after David's death, the Danes made an inroad upon the Morrisons of Morayshire, carrying off great flocks of sheep and cattle, and killing many of that clan, and escaped unpunished to their boats. They also ravaged Ireland, and almost completed the conquest of England. Many persecuted families fled before these tyrants, and took shelter in Caledonia. There is an account of one Saint Columbas, a man of great learning, having had to fly from Ireland to Caledonia, and taking refuge in a place called Saint Kilda. Saint Kilda the First was considered to be a companion of Saint Paul the Apostle, and had been at Rome to complete his learning. He wrote a great many prophecies, and was honoured in Scotland as a prophet. He told them that he was only to live thirty years from the day of his landing, and he died at the stated time, having built a hundred and thirty churches in accordance with the Chaldean creed.

About this time some of the priests of the Catholic religion got established in the Western Islands, and advised the chiefs to claim the power of life or death, like the chiefs of other nations. M'Lean of Lochbowie, the chief of the M'Leans, had been in conversation with some of the priests on the neighbouring Irish shores, who believed that the presenting of one cow would cleanse them from any sin, even murder, and make their portion in heaven sure. M'Lean had been married twice, and his second wife was a believer of this doctrine. She was very anxious to retain the possessions for her own son, though the first wife's son was alive. She advised M'Lean to enforce the power of life or death on criminals who came before his court, and then instructed a servant to put one of her cows into the firstborn's fold. But instead of doing this treacherous deed, he went to Kenneth and his family, and told him to arise and leave the island as his doom was planned, and he was certain to lose his life. He ordered his household to travel

ANCIENT HISTORY OF CALEDONIA. 121

toward the east, and to fasten his brawn stone, with which they ground their meal, on his mare's back, and to travel until it should require water, and shake the stone from its back. There he stopped and built his dwelling. The place was called Castle Brawn, the seat of the Earl of Seaford, and the brawn stone is still to be seen in the castle building. King Donald hearing of the rebellious condition of the Western Isles, took counsel of Parliament to ascertain what was to be done with this new religion, the followers of which believed in the possibility of women taking the appearance of hares and other animals, and sailing across the seas in shells, and the like nonsense. He prepared an army, but before he reached the spot, the Norwegians and Danes had broken in upon that part of the country, and plundered their lands, which caused the dispersion of the professors of this new religion. Donald held his court at Saint Lawers of Lourn, and called upon every one to come there and pay him tribute, and to make some amends for their rash steps in disturbing the peace of the realm. They submitted, and the king then marched into the Isles, but found no opposition. He replaced them in their possessions, and left a stronger army to guard them. The king saw there an exceedingly beautiful damsel named Helen M'Alpin, daughter of Malcolm M'Alpin of Isla, and married her, which strengthened the Caledonian nation, as the M'Alpins and M'Donalds were the two strongest clans, and had often intermarried before. The king then returned to Scone with his young spouse. His firstborn was called David, after the late king. The young prince unfortunately went out and eat a grey snake. The nurse being afraid to reveal the secret, hid it, and thereby left the prince in danger of being poisoned. He died during the following night. This caused Malcolm, the second son, called after his grandfather, to be the Crown Prince. Donald was very much grieved at the loss of his father's namesake, and would have deprived Malcolm of his birthright, but the voice of the nation would not allow it. The remainder of Donald's reign passed quietly, with the exception of a few inroads made by the surrounding robbers and pirates. When he was old he called the Crown Prince, Malcolm, and gave him the same counsel which he himself had received, namely, to be wise as a serpent and harmless as a dove, to be governed by Parliament, and not to draw his sword except in a just cause. He then died, and was buried at Scone, with his wife Helen, leaving the kingdom to Malcolm the First.

After Malcolm was crowned, he was married to one of his mother's clan, a daughter of Alpin M'Alpin of Dunalpin, now Duplin, but her name is not given. Their firstborn was a son, named Donald, after his grandfather. About this time England made a treaty with the Danes. One of the kings of England bound himself to subdue Caledonia, and compel them to pay tribute to the Church of Rome. The Scottish Border chiefs were warned by the gaberlunzie men that such an attack was to be made by Edward the Elder, who had been crowned king of England and Wales, by order of the Pope. The Welsh took the opportunity to rebel against the Saxon king and the power of the Pope. This held Edward back from his intended march, as the Welsh and Danes had slain above nine thousand Saxons in one camp. He lost also great numbers of his best men, who deserted his ranks and joined the Caledonians, being chiefly Gauls who had been pressed into his service by the orders of the Pope. A grant of some lands on Gala Water, near the Tweed, was made to those who had deserted the Saxons; and the Danes were allowed to fish upon the waters of Caledonia. In consequence of this treaty with the Danes, the English king contented himself with his own possessions at home, and determined to make no further attacks upon the Caledonians. Nothing more happened during the remainder of Malcolm's reign, except some acts of priestcraft which was now spreading pretty fast throughout the kingdom. King Malcolm died, leaving the crown to his son Donald.

Donald, being crowned, was married to one of the Erskines. His firstborn was called Malcolm, after his grandfather. The English still envied the prosperity of the Scots, and commenced plundering the Borders. There was a despatch sent to the king of the Scots, by Athelsten, king of England, charging him to put an end to all commerce with the Danes, and to allow the Catholic priests to traverse his country unmolested, or the Pope should be his everlasting enemy. Donald's reign became very troubled with priestcraft and witchcraft, and with priests stirring up one chief to war against the other. The confidence of the Chaldeans was completely broken, for one brother believed in the new religion, and the other still adhered to the old, so that King Donald could get no decree enforced. So he wore out his reign in a troublous state. He died, and was interred at Scone, leaving the charge of the kingdom to Malcolm, his son.

The priests said Malcolm the Second would not be a legal king except he was crowned by order of the Pope; but the king and all his rulers refused this, and he was crowned by the saints, as the former kings of Caledonia had been. Shortly after his coronation he was married to a daughter of the chief of the Macconachies. She was called Helen, the Fair Maid of Athole. She was to fulfil the prophecy which said that she was to bear three kings. Malcolm the Second had a troubled reign. He had no foreign war, but much freebooting and murder among the clans, the country being disturbed by two religious principles, so that the king and his rulers could not trust to take the field with their clans. In this condition the country remained at Malcolm's death.

As Malcolm's eldest son, Donald, died in youth, the crown fell to Duncan, who was the queen's father's name-son. He began to reign in a vigorous manner, ordering all plundering to cease, and no more poor old persons to be burnt as witches; the priests were to take no money nor cattle nor land for pardoning sin, and no men were to go about raising black mail for the Church of Rome. Many of the chiefs who believed in that faith turned the king's bitter enemies, and sought his life. The king took ill at this period, and a monk came in the character of a doctor, having been sent by the king of England as a skilful person from the French court, who could cure all diseases. He got access to the king through St. Johnstone of Perth, the king's chaplain, and ordered a small drop of thin milk porridge to be made for the king, which was immediately done. The wise Queen Helen thought this was too much kindness from an enemy, so she took the porridge that the monk had made out of the way, and substituted her own in its place. The monk waited till the king had taken his porridge, and immediately thereafter disappeared. In a little the queen went to the king's room to see if he was any better. The king said he was little better and little worse for the monk's cure. The queen, who had by this time given the porridge to a cat, to prove what was in it, replied—" My cat is not so, for it is nearly dead with poison." Malcolm, the Crown Prince, who was called Malcalm Canmore, said that when he came to the throne he would banish the last of the Pope's followers from the kingdom. The king replied that it would not be so easy to fight the enemy both abroad and at home, for it had got too great a root. The king seeing he was not very safe at Scone, retired by the advice of his councillors to Glamis. After a long and troubled reign, the monks and friars again plotted against the king's life. They hired a felon, named Macbeth, who was commander of a black-mail party, to accomplish their object. By some means he entered into the room where the king was lying ill, and the two attendants having fallen asleep, he slew them and afterwards the king, and then fled from the Castle. He afterwards usurped the crown. The king's brother-in-law, M'Duff, Thane of Fife, being enraged at the deed, raised a warlike band against Macbeth. The Erskines and the Ruthvens of Gowrie, St. Laurence of Lawers, and all the M'Larens, with a great many of the M'Alpins, were already under arms against the usurper. While M'Duff was in the field, Macbeth basely entered his house and slew his wife and children, which enraged M'Duff more than ever. The royal clans were greatly incensed against the monks and friars, but they were cautioned by St. John of St. Johnstone not to attack them, unless they wished to bring enemies at home and abroad against them, for a great many of their own people were of that persuasion. Malcolm, the Crown Prince, had to fly into Normandy, while Macbeth pursued with bitter rage all who professed the Chaldean faith; but M'Duff, whose rage was not abated, was watching his opportunity against Macbeth. He sent men to watch when he was at Dunsinane Castle, east of Perth; and he had the Erskines and the Earl of Gowrie's party all ready to avenge the deaths of his brother-in-law the king, and of his wife and family. One day, being encamped in a pass near Dunkeld, he marched toward Dunsinane. When Macbeth saw from his tower the advancing army, he thought to make his escape, but found that the Erskines and Morrisons had closed the northern pass, and the Ruthvens of Gowrie had closed the south and east. Thus the cowardly rebel was obliged to fight. M'Duff cried—" Let no innocent blood be shed for thy wicked deeds or mine, for thou art a cowardly murderer, and pierced her bosom who was as harmless as a dove." He then drew his sword in the front of his army, and ordered his men not to draw a bow until they should see what the coward would do. Macbeth in a rage, remembering the prophecy of a witch who said that he would never die by a man born of a woman, immediately sprang to the combat, cursing M'Duff, or he who should first cry—" Hold, enough !" But soon the furious and enraged M'Duff clave his helmet, crying out—" Born or not born, you'll usurp no longer." Thus fell Macbeth by the hands of M'Duff, in sight of both armies. Malcolm Canmore being proclaimed king by the royal party, one Donald Bain, taking Macbeth's party, laid claim to the crown, but he and his party had to fly.

Malcolm Canmore came home and was crowned. His queen was the first foreign queen that ever sat upon the throne of Scotland. She was named Margaret Atheling, and was a woman of great learning. She taught some ladies of her court the Latin language, and wrote in it. Malcolm was the first king of Scotland who learned to write, he having been taught at the court of Normandy. His reign was a troubled one, as there were three parties in Scotland, namely, the Romish party, Donald Bain's party, and the Royal party. Malcolm had made some promises to pay homage to the Church of Rome if he got to his throne; but instead of Margaret turning him to the Church of Rome, she turned to the Chaldean faith. Seeing that they were in danger in being so near the Abbey of Aberbrothwick, which was a nest of monks and friars, they removed westward to the Forest, now called Auchterarder, to a place called the Castle, which the nobles granted to the king, as a royal residence. On three days of each week he might have cruives on the river Earn for catching fish, and on the other four days he had to leave as much open space as a sow and twelve pigs could turn in. The king lived in a harmless manner among his subjects, and was greatly beloved. The brewer of Burnside and the king got very intimate. They often drank together, and sometimes the brewer said to the king—"If my chalks be richt, my beer is gettin' little bookit. If it had been sent to the Castle I would have three or four bickers more out of the barrel." The king having fallen behind with the brewer one pound and two pennies Scots, the king asked what favour he would do him for his money. The brewer said—"Build here a kirk, so that the folk may come to my house for their beer, and I'll not need to go to yon cold muir with my barrel and my bicker." The king granted his request, and immediately set about building the kirk, which is called the "Kirk of the Bog." The king also gave great grants of hunting ground to his foresters, and great privileges to that place now called Auchterarder.

The king of England, seeing that Malcolm disregarded his promises at the court of Normandy, by advice of the monks and friars was stirred up to war against Malcolm. He banished Malcolm's brother-in-law, Prince Atheling, from his court, and likewise prevented him from going to Normandy; so he went to king Malcolm, and succeeded in making peace between the two kings. Malcolm was summoned by the king of England to meet him at Gloucester, to sign the treaty and pay homage to him and tribute to the Church of Rome; but he refused, saying that was not a suitable place to settle such business, but on the frontiers of the two kingdoms. The king of England threatened to imprison him for breach of promise, by order of the Pope; but Malcolm escaped during the night, and went home and raised an army to stop the plunder of the king of England. Near Alnwick Castle, a monk came out with a party. The king went to make conditions, but when he took a piece of parchment from his pocket, the monk saw an opening in his armour, and stabbed him through the heart. So fell Malcolm Canmore, and his son Edmund was taken prisoner. The queen hearing the news, only survived her husband three days, and Donald Bain's party again usurped the crown. Donald, Malcolm's brother, to avenge his death, raised an army and plundered England as far as York, returning home with a heavy booty. He then commenced to rid Scotland of all English monks and such like intruders, but finding that one-half of Scotland professed what they did not perform, and seeing that treachery had entered among the clans and the Border chiefs, he threw down his sword and retired to one of the Hebrides, under an oath never more to take the field.

The Scots cast aside Donald Bain, the usurper, and placed on the throne a natural son of Malcolm, named Duncan, who was married to Margaret, the Earl of Gowrie's daughter; but in less than nine months he was cruelly murdered, and Donald Bain's party again laid claim to the crown. So grievous were the times in Scotland with bloodshed and murder that men were afraid to accept of the crown. Margaret, the widow of Duncan, retired to her father's house, and received for her son Duncan a grant of land near Dundee. This son of Margaret's was the founder of the Duncans of Camperdown.

At this time the Pope and the king of England saw an opportunity to put Scotland under their control. They sent an army, and a man named Edmund, who was said to be the true son of King Malcolm, who was slain on the Border. The Scots made no resistance, but allowed Edmund to be crowned. Immediately the country was again filled with monks and friars, and all scope given to the Church of Rome. No longer was St. John of St. John's Town Writer of the Royal Records, or Chaplain of the Royal Palace; he was banished from his church into the mountains, and so were all the saints, and every church was filled with priests, monks, and friars. Saint Michael was expelled from Dunkeld, and a bishop and abbot appointed. The whole of the Chaldean saints had to fly to the mountains, many of them to Ben-y-gloe, or the Crying Mountain, where they built a small church, the remains of which may be found to this day. The Crying Mountain was so called because people were stationed at various parts, crying—"This way, this way," to where the saints were preaching the gospel. The Abbot of Dunkeld being jealous of the Chaldean faith, raised an army by order of the king to pursue them from their mountains. The saints and all their followers had to fly to the south, and encamped at a place called Glenquich, near Loch Freuchie. A party was despatched in pursuit of them, and on a fair summer morning engaged them with an overwhelming force. In this engagement St. Fillans and St. Laurence of Lawers were slain, the Chaldeans flying further south; but still the Abbot of Dunkeld pursued. Græme Blair of Græme's Abbey, now Madderty, was pursued and followed into a house in a place called Clathy. The pursued saint took shelter underneath a bed, and the pursuers gave up the search; but a fool who had been about went to the door and cried—"The saint's below our bed." They returned and dragged him out, upon which he exclaimed—" Woe unto thee, Clathy; thou shalt never be without a fool." The Abbot and his party then went to a place called Kinkell, where they found a saint of the Chaldean faith, whom they beheaded. When they were dragging him forth he uttered the following prophecy—" Thou Kinkell may prosper and do well until they build the church across the baptismal well; then the grace of God shall decay, and from thee quickly fly away." Next day the bloodthirsty Abbot pursued the flying saints, but they were joined by Alexander, the king's uncle, and a party of other sufferers, and by M'Duff, the Thane of Fife, who resolved to give the Abbot battle. They carried all the provisions that they could find within the church and steeple of the clachan of St. David, now called Dunning. The Abbot immediately laid siege to the steeple, but was surprised by the king's uncle, Alexander, who from the swamps and woods around the small rivulet was not observed until he was close upon the Abbot's army. Seeing the Abbot raising his helmet as if to get some air for his head, Alexander immediately shot from a cross-bow an arrow which laid the Abbots pride. The battle raged across the plains, and some of Hardicanute's army joined the Abbot's army, which forced Alexander to fly to the south. M'Duff and Alexander rallied about a mile and a half from the spot, but with a long hook which the Danes used in battle, M'Duff was hooked from his horse and slain, along with the son of St. Laurence of Lawers, who was killed at the battle of Killin, near Loch Freuchie. The poor Chaldeans had to scatter in bands, not being able to withstand their enemy. All who took part in this war were banished from their estates, and many lost both head and property. Their chiefs were Donald, the Earl of Dundonald, Ruthven of Gowrie, Erskine of Mar, and a great many more of the nobles of Scotland, including William the son of St. Laurence of Lawers; and Douglas, son of the Earl of Morton, had to fly to Waldense; but the king's uncle Alexander still stood by M'Duff. During a few bloody years, Alexander, the king's uncle, and a good many more of the nobles, still adhered to the Chaldean faith. At last the king of England and the Pope planned the overthrow of the Chaldean faith, and the taking possession of the whole country. They landed a powerful army, and demanded the surrender of the nation for the deeds that Donald had done in England, after the death of his brother Malcolm. Edmund wished to accede to their request, but was opposed by his nobles. Six months of a truce was given to make up their minds, but during that period they had to support the army. Alexander, the king's uncle, lost no time in sailing to France, to acquaint all the refugees who had fled with what was about to happen. They all agreed to return and try what they could do for the liberation of the nation. They were all to assume false names so that they should not be known. The Earl of Dundonald came home under the name of Cochrane or the Company; his brother Ronald came under the name of Richard Waldense; the son of the Earl of Glasgow came under the name of Clellan; Comrie of Eagleton came under the name of De Gomrie; Ruthven of Gowrie came under the name of Ruthvine; the Erskines came under the name of Skene; William, brother of Dundonald, whose estates were in France, raised his vassals and came voluntarily home to fight the battles of his nation, and his wife, a faithful Waldense, followed him through all the struggle. Every Chaldean from the age of sixteen to seventy was called to the field. Every clan waved their own banner once more for the freedom of their country. Alexander, the king's uncle, with a small party advanced to near Balhousie Castle, which was then in possession of the Danes. They had thought themselves insulted by his denying their claim.

The Danes attempted to take Alexander and his party prisoners, but he fled upward by the south side of the Tay, and immediately the whole Danish lines were extended in battle to pursue him. Alexander and his party fell back on the main army which was stationed at a place now called Stanley, exclaiming—" We will stand on this ley." The pibroch immediately sounded the charge. Great destruction commenced on both sides, the king of the Danes, it is believed, being slain by Alexander. A stone marks the spot to this day. The Danes being driven from the solid ground into a swamp, cried out—" Luncarty, Luncarty," the name by which the place is called. The Danes were planning a retreat, but were surprised to find themselves surrounded by cavalry clad in French armour, led on by Cochrane of Dundonald. They exclaimed that the French king must have broken his treaty, as these were his soldiers, though in reality they were only the refugees who had returned from France. The Danes scattered themselves in all directions, seeking safety where best it could be found. Caledonia once more bound her laurels around her brow, and declared her independence. King Edmund fled with all his monks to the Abbey of Aberbrothwick, and Alexander was made king in his stead, being Alexander I. of Scottish history. The king decreed the forfeiture of the lands of the monks and friars, who were also ordered to leave the kingdom. The king however soon saw danger in this, as many of his nobles believed in that faith, so he agreed to a compromise that they were to pay two tributes, one to the king, and the other to the chief of the land. This brought peace for a time, till the death of Alexander, which took place in a short period, he being worn out with continual fatigue.

David, Alexander's brother, succeeded him, and had a fierce and cruel reign, as war broke out between him and England. He died of his wounds at a battle near Carlisle. Malcolm his son succeeded, but the days of the Scottish kings were and few bloody at this time. Malcolm obtained a peace for a time, getting back some of the lands and castles which his father had lost. During the reign of Malcolm little was done. He died, and was succeeded by his son William, who was a furious young man, and was named William the Lion, from the wildness of his nature. He went to war with England and was captured near Alnwick, and was carried to London; but the king of England, being a good king, gave him his freedom and the places he had lost. William in a rage made an oath that he would never lift the sword more, and shut himself up in Aberbrothwick Abbey, leaving the crown to his brother Alexander II., a man who took little interest in the nation. Monks and friars during the reign of William had got much power, and began again to take possession of land, and to lay claim to exclusive rights to fish in rivers with nets. Black-mail to the Church of Rome was generally exacted by some plundering parties. The feudal system was strong among the clans. Three crosses were erected in most places of public worship. One was for the pardoning of sin; another, made of iron, for burning heretics; and the other of wood was used for proving witches by a contrivance whereby, when the priest pulled a string, a knock was given, and the individual pronounced a witch. It was mostly during this reign that such abominations were carried on.

Alexander died, and left the crown to his son Alexander III., whose delight was more to be in company with the Chaldean Saints, than at his father's table. He joined them in their hardships. He was educated by one of the Saint Johns of St. Johnstone. He was so much beloved and admired by the nation that they called him the good Alexander. When he began to reign he gave orders that no priest or curate, monk or friar, was to fish with nets, and they were to lay no claim to the water, or to prohibit people from fishing. They were also ordered to pay the tribute they had agreed on in the reign of Alexander I. He reinstated the Saint Johnstones in their ancient occupation of king's writers and preachers to the palace, which offended the monks and all of their persuasion so much that they planned the ruin of the king. The Norwegians were to get one-third of the kingdom, and the Danes and the English the other two-thirds, and the Chaldeans were to be expelled. The Danes were to enter from the east, the Norwegians from the west, and the English from the south. The king was surprised by a message that the Norwegians and Irish had landed at Largs, and by another message that the Danish fleet was lying off Montrose. The king took counsel of his faithful St. Johnstone as to what was to be done. He was advised to fight the first landed, and leave plenty at home to guard the east coast and arm the Douglases with authority to watch the Border, the Western Highlanders having to fight their own battle led on by the king. The king stirred up one-third of his nation, and marched to Largs. He was supported by the Earl of Glasgow. The battle was planned to put Douglas' and Montgomery's horse behind the hill to watch their opportunity. M'Donald of the Isles commanded the Highlanders, who immediately drew themselves up in battle array across the beach. The king with the men of Fife took up a position on the right wing. The clans were to attack at the first sound of the king's horn. The engagement raged fiercely on both sides. Two blasts of the king's trumpet brought forward Montgomery's horse, who made great slaughter among the enemy. The M'Donalds made an opening for Douglas' horse to advance, which they did on hearing three blasts on the king's horn. By this time the Norwegians were endeavouring to get into their boats, but they found that Black M'Phee from the island of Colzie had done great damage to their ships during the engagement. Haco the king fell into the hands of Alexander, but he asked his liberty, which was granted on condition that he should never more invade Scotland. He retired to the Orkneys, and died of a broken heart at the loss of his army and his fleet.

The Danes, having landed in the east, were opposed by M'Duff and the Earl of Gowrie. They fought a battle near Glammis. A stone marks the spot with this inscription—"Here lies the king of Denmark, and forty thousand of his men." The king of England had advanced as far as Morpeth, to make the attack from the southern side, but was met by Douglas. A heavy skirmish took place, which resulted in the king of England flying towards York. Douglas in the usual fashion plundered all the northern counties of England, and returned with a heavy booty. The king remained at Dunfermline, owing to the illness of his son, the Crown Prince. The marriage of his daughter Margaret with Eric king of Norway was delayed from the same cause. The Crown Prince died, which was a great loss to Scotland, as he appeared to possess the virtues of his father. The marriage of Margaret to the king of Norway was now celebrated, which formed a bond of peace between the two nations. Alexander emptied all the churches of monks and friars, and appointed Chaldean saints to the churches. The king having been engaged one day in Kirkcaldy, placing a Chaldean minister, was beset by assassins on his way home, and was thrown with his horse over a precipice between Burntisland and Kinghorn. The people had heard the blast of the king's horn, but paid little attention to it, which gave the name of Kinghorn to that place. So fell Alexander, who was the last of the M'Donald race of kings. He was remarkable for his open and generous heart, as well as for his bravery in the field.

The crown now fell to Alexander's granddaughter, who by her mother's death was heir to the crowns of both Scotland and Norway. She was called the Fair Maid of Norway. At this time the king of England saw a fair opening to make himself a great monarch. He proposed a marriage between the Maid of Norway and his son, which grieved the Scottish nation very much. They abhorred the idea of being ruled by an English king, and being again over-run with priestcraft. This fine scheme was, however, thwarted by the death of the Maid of Norway before the marriage could be celebrated. The succession to the crown was now open, and numerous claimants appeared. Saint Johnstone was again banished from the Palace.

[THE END.]

www.ingramcontent.com/pod-product-compliance
Lightning Source LLC
Chambersburg PA
CBHW030400170426
43202CB00010B/1435